MEMORIES OF

Quinton

MEMORIES OF
Quinton

Bernard J. Taylor

TEMPUS

Frontispiece A wartime fancy-dress party.

First published 2004

Tempus Publishing Limited
The Mill, Brimscombe Port,
Stroud, Gloucestershire, GL5 2QG

British Library Cataloguing in Publication Data.
A catalogue record for this book is available from the British Library.

ISBN 0 7524 3306 7

Typesetting and origination by Tempus Publishing Limited
Printed in Great Britain

Contents

Acknowledgements

I would like to extend my heartfelt thanks to everyone whose words, stories and photographs helped in the compilation of this book, for their time, generosity and warmth, and indeed, for their responses to my questions and requests for interviews.

They are as follows: Anthony Armstrong, Joyce Barber, Mary and Lawrence Basterfield, Margaret Bate, Marjorie Berry, Joyce and John Birch, Geoff Broughton, Mrs Burden, Denis Colclough, Delia Compton, Eileen Collins, Harry Cook, Daisy Cooper, Helen Cooper, Harry Cottrell, Susie Coxill, Miss Cutler, Audrey Davies, Clive Davies, Mary Davis, Lucy Dearn, Bill Deeley, Irene Devereux, Marilyn Ditch, Lynne Dyson, Winifred Eccles, Brian Gastinger, Elsie Hall, Valerie Hanson, Vivienne Harris, Gwen Harwood, Reg Hewitt, Mrs D. Hobbs, Rod Homer, Nora Hyett, Geoffrey Johnson, Harvey Johnson, H.C. Johnson, David B. Jones, Gladys Jones, Stuart Jones, Sheila Joyner, Dorothy Kenning, E. Kesterton, Phil Lamb, Vivian Lawton, Stella Linnington, Keith McDonald, Andrew Maxam, Dorothy Mason, Eileen and Brian Lee, Susan Newland, Bryan Palser, Georgina Prescott, Derek Price, Betty Rose, John Round, P. Round, John Scanlon, June Shepherd-Drew, Bryan Slim, Derek Smart, Brian Smith, Smith Bros (Quinton) Ltd, Joan Smith, Ron Smith, Margaret Statham, Jean Sunderland, Charlotte Tate, D. Timms, Stella Trigg, Mary Watson, Dinah Willetts, Horace Wilson, Christine Windsor, Gertrude Wood and Derek Woodward.

I hope I have not failed to omit anyone from the above list but please accept my apologies should someone's contribution have slipped my memory. On many occasions, someone has approached me at an exhibition or talk, or in the street and has thrust an envelope or package of information into my hand; I think I have made note of their names but anyone who knows me should realise I am not infallible.

Permission to use the photographs and recordings has been sought where it has been possible to establish the copyright holder, but apologies are extended for any inadvertent breach of copyright.

I would also wish to extend my condolences to the families of those named above who have sadly died since I conducted my interviews; their memory lives on.

Foreword

Since time immemorial people have told stories. They have told stories to explain big matters such as life, creation and the world, they have told stories to explain that which they could not understand in nature and men and women, and they have told stories about their own experiences, the lives of their families and the deeds of those long dead. In West Africa, storytelling is an art practised by skilled men called *griots*. Through their storytelling, they pass on the history of their people orally and it is said that a library burns to the ground when a *griot* dies. Similarly, in the west of Ireland, the consciousness of the people and the happenings of those long since gone is passed on by men called *seannachaí*. Sadly these *seannachaí* are declining in numbers and influence as Ireland too falls under the thrall of a way of life dedicated to today and tomorrow and to an aversion to that which is slow and deliberate as opposed to fast and reactive.

Within the Western world as a whole there seems to be an aversion to recognising the importance of oral history and to valuing historical evidence passed on by word of mouth. It is an aversion inextricably bound up with class. For centuries, official history was passed on by those who were literate and the great majority of those who could read and especially write were from the wealthier classes. Thus there arose the belief that 'proper' history is to be found only in documents, whilst the spoken word is useful only as colour and anecdotes. That presumption is a fallacy. The father of written history, Herodotus, at the beginning of his work on the wars between the ancient Greeks and Persians, wrote compellingly and truthfully, 'I have written down all that I have heard'.

Oral history is as good a source as any other piece of historical evidence and it should be handled in the same way – carefully, thoughtfully and sympathetically. Wherever possible it should be used in conjunction with other forms of evidence, but unlike those other forms of evidence, oral history powerfully calls out to us in its own right as the thoughts, attitudes and beliefs of one person and of his or her forebears. I became a historian because I harked back to the stories of my family and because I read the stories that had been written down from the spoken word about heroes such as Robin Hood, Finn McCool, Hereward the Wake and others. Never diminish the importance of the spoken word in passing on history. That is a trap that Bernard Taylor has not fallen into. Through his interviews and the stories of those with whom he has spoken, he has given value to those who may have been lost to formal history and he has ensured that they and their people shall live on. I congratulate him on his achievement.

Professor Carl Chinn MBE

Introduction

I was born in Smethwick in 1948 and lived there, or Bearwood, until I was married to my darling wife, Iris, in 1975. Since then, I have been a Quintonian and have shared my life and experiences with the people who live there.

History has always been a family interest, in fact my daughter Kay obtained her Bachelor of Arts in History at the University of Birmingham. My passion for local history began about eight years ago; I love looking through books and discovering how life was in the early part of the 1900s. A lot of pleasure is derived from examining old photographs and postcards which depict the life and times experienced by many all those years ago. I am fascinated by the comparison of how areas look now compared to many years ago, not just for this area but other areas that I am familiar with. My first project when Quinton Local History Society began in 1999 was a 'Now and Then' display in time for the Millennium. In fact, Chapter One of my first book, *Images of England, Quinton*, was entitled 'Now and Then'.

Oral history is another topic of local history that is very important. The world in which we live today has become a very visual one; the ability to talk to each other and to express through speech how we feel and our experiences in life seems to be a thing of the past. I would say that Professor Carl Chinn, Birmingham's own community historian, has had an influence on my feelings and many others associated with the field of local history. Carl's passion and enthusiasm is infectious. He has the tremendous ability to describe what he sees in such a way that those listening feel that they are there. Carl is a friend and I am proud to be associated with him. It is very important for readers to understand what is meant by oral history before they begin to read this book; they need to understand how the concept sets it apart from other historical disciplines.

This book is a collection of peoples' memories and reminiscences of the experiences they had whilst living and working in this area. History books are a collection of factual research, the gathering of facts and dates, supported by references to extensive and painstaking research. The recording of oral history follows the same painstaking research but unfortunately this is where the similarity ends – oral history is dependent on memory, which, as you are no doubt aware, has a habit of occasionally playing strange tricks on us all. We all believe our recollection of the past is perfect and we are adamant that our thoughts are the correct ones; faces, names, dates and times are all a vivid picture in our minds. We can give really accurate accounts of events without a moment's pause, but unfortunately we must realise that whilst the gist of an event or incident is relatively simple to recall, the actual facts and specifics regarding that event can be flawed with error. If you are looking for accurate historical fact, you will rarely find it in oral history. However, if you are looking for an evocative recollection of events, people, places and life, you will find it in oral history. In this book, you can see and read about life in Quinton and its nearby areas. These memories depict our families' lives in the early part of the 1900s. In oral history, you will feel the joy and sadness, the highs and lows of family and public events as though through the eyes of the people who lived them.

This book is a compilation of interviews that were recorded with a small pocket tape recorder or with the help of my good friend Paul Baker, using his sophisticated digital equipment. The interviews have been placed on CD-Rom. When time permits, these will be edited and made available to a wider listening audience. However, at present, I do at least know that for posterity I have digitally saved the memories of these Quintonians. This book also includes passages from the society's quarterly journal, *The Quinton Oracle*. This journal is a means of making those society members who are not able to attend meetings because of distance feel part of the society.

The interviews, passages and stories have been collected over the last four years. From the first day the society began, I have wanted to publish something which records people's memories. I have visited many homes and would like to take this opportunity to thank everyone concerned for their hospitality and warmth. Group and one-to-one interviews have taken place in other venues. During these interviews, everyone has been warm, friendly and informative. Sometimes they have shared with me their innermost secrets, followed by the comment 'but please don't record that'. I promise them all, discretion has been observed at all times.

It was a pleasure to conduct these interviews. I found it quite amazing how many times I heard the words, 'But what will I talk about for an hour?' or 'I am sure you won't find what I have to tell you very interesting'. Well, let me tell you all, I did find what you had to tell me very interesting and I am sure everyone else will too. At the end of almost every interview, the comment was 'Oh! Is it that time already?'

This book is about oral history, but what would a local history book be without the odd photograph or two? Most of the images in this book have not been published before – I apologise for any that have but I only included them when I felt it necessary to depict the story being told. My thanks go to all those people who loaned the photographs to me to copy, and for their permission to include them in this book. I know how sentimental people can be about these prized and precious possessions, but I have always believed that it is more rewarding to share a photograph with others than to hoard it away for personal satisfaction.

The most difficult part of oral history is transcribing the recordings. I have tried to use the words of the interviewees as much as possible, as I believe that the greatest importance lies in what was said and certainly how it was said. On occasions, however, it is almost impossible not to have to add or delete the odd word or two, if only just for clarity.

The compilation of this book has been a labour of love. It has allowed me to meet many people and to somehow get under the surface, to try and relive their lives and understand their triumphs, their loves and their hardships. I hope that you enjoy reading it as much as I have enjoyed writing it.

Finally, I wish to dedicate this book to the memory of my mom and dad, Ivy and Jim Taylor, without whose devotion, love and guidance I wouldn't be who, what or where I am today; God bless you both.

Bernard J. Taylor

one

Childhood Days

Odeon's Tuppenny Crush

Saturday morning with money in my pocket, earned from running all sorts of errands, off I would go to the Odeon's Tuppenny Crush', 2d to get in downstairs but if full the empty balcony at 4d was too expensive.

The lights would dim, a cartoon, a feature film and ice cream at 1d from a young lady usherette standing just in front of the stage with the spotlight beaming on to her.

Finally the serial, which always ended in a gripping ordeal, we couldn't wait for next Saturday to come along.

Miss Gladys Jones

Annuals were always 12s 6d

I am a good friend of Peter Alford; as a lad, his father would buy him an annual every year.

When he looked, he had a lot from the 1950s to the 1960s and every one of them was priced 12s 6d, the price didn't rise but nowadays everything goes up all the time.

Workers have changed, people didn't go on strike for more money in those days, whereas nowadays they go on strike at the drop of a hat. Things were different then because you could leave work on the Friday and get another job on the Monday.

When I was fourteen, I started in engineering then I was called up to the Army. After I came out, I did some painting and decorating. I started working for myself in 1955 and did so for about forty years or so. I was more than happy, never made a fortune but I was content. A fair day's pay for a fair day's work.

Now it's funny you should say about prices; I've got a billhead dated about 1908 from a firm in Carver Street in Birmingham. The firm came here and decorated, well whitewashed, the hall, kitchen and cellar for 9s 3d. They would have come from Carver Street by horse and cart – there were no vans in those days – which was a journey of about 12 miles there and back, and the bill also included materials.

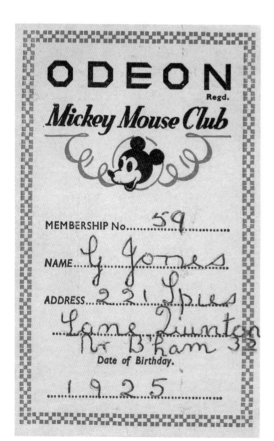

The Odeon cinema in Wolverhampton Road's 'Mickey Mouse Club Card' belonging to Gladys Jones in 1925.

Harry Cook

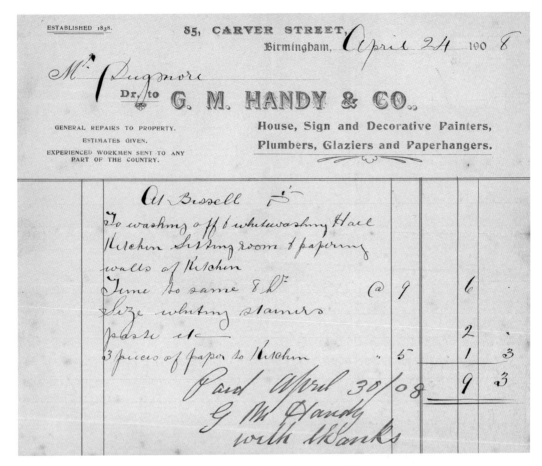

An invoice from G.M. Handy & Co. for decorating work at Bissell Street in 1908.

Boys in short trousers

We are losing sight of many precious customs and traditions, such as the fair. It usually rained, but that didn't matter as I would wear my old mac, the one that touched the tops of my wellies. I could spend my hard-earned few coppers on the many stalls: roll the ball (2d), throw the loop over the goldfish bowl (3d), but I never managed to win one. Throw a soft ball (3d) to win a double-jointed doll, dressed in a cheap pink cotton dress; her limbs would disintegrate in a few days. After pink candyfloss on a stick, a toffee apple or a roasted potato which was nearly always partly raw, I still had a few coppers left for a go on the swing boats.

They were simple pleasures, but we were happy and we always had our dreams.

Another simple thing I remember now: boys always wore short trousers whatever the weather, until they were fourteen when they started work.

Miss Gladys Jones

1st Quinton Boys' Brigade

In 1937, at the age of twelve, I joined the Boys' Brigade. I became an officer on 15 September 1947, a post awarded by the Church.

The 1st Quinton Co. Boys' Brigade met in the Methodist church in College Road in

1st Quinton Boys' Brigade in 1944, photographed outside Carters Lane Baptist church.

Carters Lane Youth Club trip to the Malvern Hills in 1950-51.

Quinton every Friday night between 7 p.m. and 9.30 p.m. The uniform was a white haversack with a leather belt and brass buckle and forage cap. The Brigade badge was a star with 'B.B' in letters across it. Our leader was W. Rollason.

The evening consisted of drilling, which we did in fours, then physical training and first aid. We did badge work; it was very difficult to get a badge and you had to do weeks, even years, of hard work to attain one. The badges were diamond shaped. I have here a long-service award which was given after four years.

In 1943, we amalgamated with the 2nd Quinton Co. at Carters Lane Baptist, and moved our headquarters there. The flag was a red St George Cross on a white background with the Boys' Brigade emblem in the centre.

I also have fond memories of being a member of Carters Lane Youth Club.

Reg Hewitt

Vinegar on draught

I grew up in that corner of Quinton near the water tower and have very fond memories of Quinton, from being a Christmas postman round the Hollybush area when I was a student, to helping with jumble sales when in the Scouts at St Faith and St Lawrence – it was nearer than Christ Church.

Also I recall when the plane crashed at White Road in the later days of the war, the little farm by the Beech Tree and so on.

One memory I have is of the basket makers in Birch Road, buying apples for 3d per pound from the old ladies who lived nearby, and the off-licence with draught vinegar at 4d per pint.

My home turf was near the junction of Castle Road West and Birch Road. We lived on what would have been Christ Church's Quinton glebe lands in the days of Revd Compton.

I recall my father's comment: 'Time to pay the cricketer his ground rent'.

Bryan Slim

Memories of Granny Jones

One of my earliest memories of Granny Jones's house was the sticky flypaper which always hung over the centre of the table in the living room. It was always black with flies and seldom changed.

I also remember the battery-operated radio which was always turned on, but so faint you had to put your ear right up against the speaker to hear anything. Granny Jones was always seated on the couch and I never saw her stand up.

The house was semi-detached, three storeys high and had a large bay window to the front room, which suggests it may have been a shop at one time. The toilet was outside; I can't remember if it was a chain-pull lavatory or a long drop, but I remember the very large wooden seat. It was shared with the other house and was a long walk from the house.

I remember the black cast-iron water pump in the centre of the yard. At the top of the yard, actually adjacent to the neighbours' house but not used by them, was the brewhouse. It was quite a large building with a high ceiling and whitewashed walls; there was a built-in boiler in one corner and a cold tap and stone sink and very little else. Granddad Jones used to do shoe repairs when he was at home. He always sat in the doorway of the brewhouse on an old kitchen chair with the cobbler's last on a box between his knees. He had a very long moustache and he always had a mouthful of nails and would spit out one nail at a time between his whiskers. I was always fascinated by this procedure when I was a young child.

Left Maud Jones in the back yard of 845 Hagley Road West in the 1940s. The Essoldo cinema can be seen in the centre of the photograph.

Below Pat Jones taking a tricycle ride in the early 1940s; the old brewhouse can be seen in the background.

The living room was quite small and most of it was taken up by a large table with a chenille cloth. There was a black-leaded range with a side oven and an open fire with a large black kettle always on the boil. There was a fire in the grate all year round. There was also a gas cooker in a very dark corner, squeezed in between the range and the wooden door to the stairs. I remember going up the dark wooden stairs on hands and knees and up a second flight to the attic. Mom told me that she, Florrie, and later Louie, all slept in the one double bed. The living room was lit by a gaslight that gave an eerie yellow light and always made a purring noise.

There was a pegged rag rug in front of the fire which was made by cutting up old woollen clothes into strips and, with a dolly peg cut in half, the strips were pushed through a piece of hessian backing and back to the front again to form a tuft on the top. Hundreds of strips were inserted to form a very attractive rug. The only drawback was they held the dirt and were very heavy to shake.

Margaret Statham

Scrattings with salt and vinegar

Half way up the High Street on the left was the general store owned by the Miss Round sisters: 'Please can we have a halfpennyworth of mixed sweets, and any chance of a piece of cheese left over from the wooden board and cheese cutter on the counter?' Another call would be to Phillip Hill's fish and chip shop, half way up the High Street on the right: 'Could we have a bag of scrattings with salt and vinegar?'– free of course!

During the autumn, we went blackberry picking and had a large basin full to the brim to take round to Dr Young's, opposite our cottage in Spies Lane. We would be given 6d and a large piece of home-made cake – such bliss. Then to the Chocolate Box on the corner of Shenstone Valley Road. Les, the owner's son, would let us have a pick from the 1d and 2d box. At the same time, we would place a penny or two on the Christmas card saver for Mom's present.

Quite often when we crept under the hedges of the local orchards, Pardoe, the local bobby, was waiting for us. We used to run like hell with the 'goodies' tucked up in our thick navy blue knickers, the apples would roll around and sometimes drop out, but we escaped.

The traders used to call round the roads selling their wares. The milk had to be collected in a jug from Albert Porter, after he had returned from Bearwood with his pushcart.

Hobbs called round in his horse and cart with firewood (we gathered ours free from the hedgerows) paraffin, candles, scrubbing brushes etc.

The bread man delivered two or three times a week from Blackheath and there was Shuker the greengrocer. All us kids looked forward to a ride on the back of his cart and asking for any 'specs' [speckled fruit].

The local chimney sweep that called during the summer months also doubled up as the coal man. Sometimes we couldn't afford the sweep so we would tie a holly branch to a rope, climb onto the roof and pull it through. Sometimes the branch detached itself from the rope and the living room got covered with black chimney dust.

I remember collecting newspapers from the big houses to cut into squares – make a hole in the corner for the string to go through and hang behind the toilet door; none of your fancy white toilet paper in our house – we couldn't afford that!

Miss Gladys Jones

Muffin the Mule

My mother had a friend with a large-screen 12in television set – a delightful lady who in appearance was very much like Mrs Fox out of *Dad's Army*. She suggested that my mother brought my sister and I to watch a programme specifically for children. I was looking forward to seeing this programme on a large screen but it turned out to be one of life's great disappointments.

The lady in question was very house proud and exceedingly fussy. We were asked to remove our shoes and made to sit correctly on the settee. The programme we had come to watch was one of the most boring programmes I could have imagined. It was entitled *Muffin the Mule*, and I believe it was presented by Annette Mills. The broadcast only lasted about ten minutes but then we had to sit for a further length of time whilst we ate cake and drank a cup of tea. She was so fussy that my sister and I were frightened to move in case any crumbs from the cake fell on the floor or, worse, we spilt some tea.

Keith McDonald

Pear Tree Cottage

I happen to be one of the young ones who were born at World's End in 1921 at a place called Pear Tree Cottage. It was one of two cottages owned by my grandparents, Thomas and Elizabeth Cox. The cottages were sold in around 1925.

My sisters went to Quinton School by the old Quinton cemetery. They had a very long walk to school up the country lane. The lane was really desolate and narrow with a stream that ran there, and open fields for miles around. We used to paddle in this stream in the summer and pick daisies for daisy chains; this is how I come to have the first of my names.

Opposite our two cottages, there used to be a small dairy called Burton's, and you could always see the big milk churn outside. I believe a lady called Mrs Pettifer lived higher up the lane in a small cottage. She was always baking and would give my sister and I some home-made cakes and pies. A little higher up still, I think there were three or four cottages. A lady called Katie Wise lived in one, hence my second name became Katie, because she knew my family.

Our Saturday treat was a trip to Bearwood shops; I would be in the perambulator with my parents and my sisters walking. On our journey we would pass by Underhill's Cottage where you could get sweets, pop and papers. The cottages stood opposite the site of what was the Hollybush Hotel, and later Jeffersons. We would then walk up the long hill, past the original Hollybush Pub and allotments, straight down the Hagley Road to the Kings Head where the old trams from Birmingham used to turn round, and then down to the Bear Inn, as we knew it. My sisters used to call the Bearwood Road to the Dog Inn their 'monkey run'. Why, I do not know, but it was there you would find the local lads to meet and chat to.

Daisy Cooper (*née* Preece)

A Christmas sunbeam

Christ Church Junior School staged a Christmas play each year. One year I was a sunbeam with a piece of yellow cloth for a cloak, 6d a yard from Lewis's in Birmingham. Because it was too small for me, I had to stand in the back row so I couldn't be seen. My Christmas treat was a trip to Lewis's to see Father Christmas – 2s for a present wrapped in paper, pink for a girl and blue for a boy – then a walk around the shops. The harvest festival with the vicar, Revd Palmer, was also at

The tram stops at the Bearwood terminus in 1918.

Christ Church; all proceeds were taken to the old children's hospital.

The summer festival was in the grounds of the vicarage with dancing around the maypole, but how were us 'Spies Lane kids' to take part when our parents did not have the money to buy the white socks and dresses and the nice clean shoes? We had to be content with hide 'n' seek. If we got dirty, we wiped ourselves with dock leaves 'to get rid of the muck', then went home for a wash in the big tub in front of the coal fire. Just before bed, we had a bowl of Mom's home-made stew made with local rabbits, roasted in apple sauce, or shin beef cooked with fresh vegetables from Shuker's cart and some pearl barley lentils. We cleaned our teeth with salt on our finger.

My fondest memories of my mom's cooking were faggots, peas and mashed potato in front of the Dutch oven in front of the fire, where the sausages were cooked. If we were lucky, we could dip the bread in the fat that dropped from the meat.

The tablecloth was old newspaper, apart from special occasions such as birthdays, christenings, funerals and the like when we had a white tablecloth and salmon sandwiches – a real luxury. Our front door was never locked as there was nothing to pinch. My dear mother cleaned and scrubbed floors on her hands and knees in the new houses built in Gower Road and Shenstone Valley Road for the princely sum of 2s 6d. These houses had one of these wonderful things called a bathroom and a kitchen with a cooker.

Miss Gladys Jones

Quinton's first youth club

From mother's experiences with the Co-op, she decided to start a youth club, held every

Elizabeth Compton wins first prize in the fancy dress competition.

Friday evening, initially in the old Co-op shop on Hagley Road West in Quinton.

Children from the village as it then was and also from further afield came along to enjoy this new venture. A representative committee was formed from amongst the older ones and a programme of events was set out. The usual games were played, with an emphasis on teamwork and a little friendly competition, songs were taught, talents were encouraged and outings were arranged.

In summertime there was an outing to a place of interest. I particularly remember going by bus to Hagley and from there walking all the way to Harvington Hall. Most of the children were aged between seven and fourteen; they came from lowly working-class homes and the club was an important part of their life.

One year, the grandmother of one young lad was so appreciative of the pleasure he had

from the club that she surprised us all at Christmas by treating everyone to a seat at the pantomime in Birmingham, an event never before experienced by many.

By this time, the war was over, celebrations passed and life, though still hard, was returning to normality. As transport became easier, we entered into competition with branches of youth clubs from other districts. I remember a swimming gala, held at Woodcock Street Baths in Birmingham. We were only a small group representing Halesowen and Hasbury. Ten Acres and Stirchley were the favourites to win but gradually we built up the points one by one; the excitement was intense and in the end we took the honours!

As the years slipped by, there were now other attractions for young folk to pursue and gradually numbers dwindled down to a few old faithfuls. The old Co-op shop was needed for retailing again so the club had to move to new premises in the basement of an old church in Halesowen, near to the then traffic lights at the bottom of Mucklow Hill. We set about cleaning the bare cobwebbed room and tried very hard to start again but the atmosphere was not the same. Finally, reluctantly, the club closed.

Mrs Vivienne Harris (*née* Jacomb)

Cow manure for sale

The cows and sheep came up and down the lane, the cows twice daily to be milked at the local farms. The animals were quite profitable to us kids. The manure left following the cows' visits would be collected in galvanised buckets and sold for 6d a full bucket and 3d for half a bucket. It was hard work, carrying the full buckets, but well worth it just to put a few pence on the Christmas card saver or buy a few sweets.

Miss Gladys Jones

Rats from cornricks

As a lad I lived at 1 Bissell Street. I remember the Wesleyan chapel which stood next to the Toll House on the corner of the Hagley Road and College Road. I also recall the farm where the King's Highway now stands but that spot has very special memories for me and my friends, the lads of the village. We enjoyed killing the rats with a stick that issued from the cornricks whenever the farmer was thrashing his wheat – happy days!

Opposite Stoney Lane stood a number of old cottages. In one lived a Mr Detheridge who I think was the sexton of Christ Church in Quinton. Incidentally, for a short period, I was a chorister there.

The staff of Yates builders taken at the premises in High Street.

Mr Masters, the fireman, lived in Bissell Street. The handpump and other fire-fighting equipment were stored in the fire station in Ridgacre Road. Periodically, a visit was made to the Masters' home by a two-wheeled vehicle which was always drawn by lovely grey horses. We were always told those visits were by officials from Birmingham on tours of inspection to examine the fire-fighting equipment. I cannot remember any out-standing fires which Fireman Masters was ever called upon to attend except for some which arose as a result of the burning out of wasps nests.

The premises at the corner of High Street and Bissell Street were used as a home brewery and in the yard was a large and barred type of cage in which there was a large St Bernard dog. A family called Yates kept these premises at one time. It was quite a common practice, until the First World War at any rate, for the owners of public houses to brew their own ale, and there were many families like the Yates's doing this throughout the district.

On the opposite corner was a house. The occupiers, whose name was Powell, kept a few chickens and a pig in their garden. I remember attending one or two of their 'pig-killings' and helping to draw the chitterlings.

Harvey Johnson

Ridgacre Methodist Girls' Brigade

The Sunday school of Ridgacre Methodist church met in the community centre. It was there when I joined in 1946. The person in charge was Mr Green, and Mr Yates assisted him. A few years later, there was a parade of the Sunday school to the new church in World's End Lane.

The Girls' Life Brigade, now the Girls' Brigade, was formed around 1950. The captain was Miss Green and the officer was Miss Sheila Oglesby. Miss Oglesby lived at the top of White Road and her parents kept the jeweller's shop on Hagley Road. Three young ladies who joined the company were Barbara Lewis, Pat Perks and myself, Dinah Hunt. Over the years we moved through the ranks and I eventually became the captain. In 1967, I moved over to the Boys' Brigade.

Mrs Dinah Willetts (*née* Hunt)

Progress!

My memories of Spies Lane in the summer of 1930 were of horse and carts; the branches of the trees overhung the road and would touch you as you walked along at twilight. One's imagination ran wild with witches and ghosts. We all had our own witch in the area and ours was such a kind, wonderful lady; her name is a secret and will remain so.

I remember when they cut those trees down. Progress: we were to have real light to take the place of the oil lamp standing in the middle of the table, also gas, and water from a tap. The men came and widened Spies Lane. They dug, by hand, trenches about 2 yards wide. These would be a great source of amusement for us kids. When it rained, because of the many springs around Quinton, the trenches would fill with water and we could go canoeing down them on the tree trunks.

When darkness descended, a night-watchman came and lit his brazier. Sometime in the evening he would disappear as one of his visits was to the black and white Old Royal Oak public house on the corner of Spies Lane and Carters Lane. Also on the corner of Carters Lane was a small farm and in the front parlour of the farmhouse was a shop – I recall that the shop was always very smelly.

When the nightwatchman returned from the pub, just a little bit merry, he would find

The 40th Company of the Girls' Brigade parading from Ridgacre Road to Stoney Lane then on to Quinton Methodist church in 1950.

us kids huggled together in the hut keeping warm by the fire.

At last we had gas and water from a tap. However, just like today, the workmen came back a few years later. This time they dug up all the trenches to put electricity into the houses. We missed the lamplighter, who would arrive regularly each evening on his bicycle, to check the gas lamp outside our cottage.

Miss Gladys Jones

Unlucky No.13

We moved to 11 World's End Lane when the higher numbers were still in the course of construction. Our next-door neighbour, Peter Hoult, lived at No.15 because the use of 13 was avoided in the area.

At the time, Ridgacre Road, a dual lane, was confined to the southernmost lane. The other lane, unfinished, was used by the RAF, who operated a barrage balloon in the field between World's End Lane and Ridgacre Lane. The RAF used to park a low-loader there sometimes, with portions of recovered aircraft. I remember putting my hand into a cavity in a section of wing and removing spent cartridges and clips as used in a machine gun. I took them home to conceal under my bedroom floor (over the entrance porch) where I had discovered a loose board.

My grandfather, a policeman, moved to the rural area of Quinton on a doctor's advice due to my father's tendency towards breathlessness. This was good advice as my father lived to the age of seventy-seven. At the time of the move

Higgins Lane in 1934.

he was aged about five. My neighbour Peter Hoult and I attended Woodhouse Road Junior School.

I saw the name Francis Brett-Young mentioned in your Oracle. Our local library in Dublin had no record of the author, who was a favourite of my mother. I recall one title, Mr Lucton's Freedom.

Geoffrey Johnson

Children's Saturday Club

In the late 1930s and during the war years I used to attend the Children's Saturday Club at the Warley Odeon. You paid 6d to sit downstairs and 9d in the balcony. On your birthday you received a card and were allowed in free of charge. I think your names were flashed on the screen. I used to attend the Saturday film shows with my friend Graham Potts; we used to come home from the Odeon via all the right of ways between the rear of the semi-detached houses in Quinton Lane and World's End Avenue. In this right of way was a spring of water and we enjoyed 'damming up' the subsequent stream, although our mothers were not very happy when we arrived home wet and muddy but happy. One Saturday morning when I called for my friend Graham, his irate mother came to the door: 'Graham can't come out today, he left the plug in the wash-basin, the water has overflowed and come through the kitchen ceiling, so he's got to clean the fowl pen out!'

Bryan Palser

The 'old pushchair' jaunts

On bank holidays, the gang would go walking to Clent. We took the old pushchair for carrying things and rides down the hills. Then we took it in turns coming home at night, no lights in those days only the stars and the moon to escort you home.

Mom would give us some jam sandwiches, cold tea and some yellow kali powder mixed with water.

We would come home late in the evening tired but content.

We didn't know words like 'abuse' or 'stress' or what was happening in the outside world, Dudley, Harborne, Wolverhampton, London – where?

We had no radio or television so our imagination had to work overtime, usually on the ghosts around every corner up in the churchyard and when we were walking around Halesowen Manor Abbey.

A Sunday night treat was walking through the farm fields to the Beech Tree public house, picking watercress on the way from Watery Lane, calling at the Hollybush pub for a rest on the grass and collecting any cigarette cards from the customers.

Then, after a run around, we would ride home on the top deck of the no. 9 bus. The thrill of a lifetime was an aeroplane that operated for a while in the field at the back of our house; it was 5s for a trip over Quinton but that was only for the rich.

Miss Gladys Jones

An almighty rumble

My introduction to Quinton was in 1935 when my father took over the premises known then as The Grange Sweet Shop in Frankley Avenue.

This area, even back in those days, was actually in the Borough of Halesowen, but as it enjoyed a Birmingham B32 postcode and had a Birmingham WOO 2109 telephone number, it was always known as Quinton. At the time of moving, I was just seven years old and my sister Beryl was then twelve. We moved in at about midday, and our parents Billy and Elsie suggested that Beryl and I took a walk to find our bearings round the locality whilst they got the furniture installed.

We set off down Frankley Avenue just before 1 p.m. and had not got very far when we heard this almighty rumble in the distance. Thinking it was thunder, we ran back home as quickly as we could.

We later learned this used to happen at the same time every weekday. It was the blasting from Samson's Quarry up at Rowley Regis. In those days other familiar sounds were to be heard, the most memorable being the works 'bull' at Somers works on Mucklow hill. This factory also had a very large steam hammer which could be heard for miles around.

Another noise was the trains, which we could sometimes hear climbing up the steep incline from Old Hill to Blackheath. They used to whistle before entering the tunnel.

Clive Davies

Earn a penny?

Opposite our house lived Dr Young, the father of Brett Young; he was the medical officer of health for Halesowen. Dr Young's housekeeper would call out 'Who wants to earn a penny?' and I could run the fastest so I would collect the post from the housekeeper and run to the no. 9 bus in Ridgacre Road at nine o'clock in the evening.

The bus would have a special pillarbox fixed to the handrail on the entrance; delivery would be in London next day at 9 a.m. The cost would be about 1½d or 2d.

Billy Davies at his Grange Stores in Frankley Avenue in the 1950s.

If you wanted sweets then you did errands such as apple- or blackberry-picking, would collect food from the grocers or vegetables from the greengrocers in College Road almost opposite the back of the Toll House, or carry paraffin for the table oil lamps.

One of my errands would be to collect the pensioners' beer from the New Inns but on my way there I would go into Quinton Park, have a few goes on the swings and a few runs around the shelter. Then I would go up to the fire station, a small red hut, to look at the fire engine. The New Inns public house was in Ridgacre Road, about five houses from the bottom of High Street. I would collect the beer in a jug but if I took bottles, a label was placed over the bottle stopper, so us youngsters wouldn't drink it.

But I used to have a swig out of the jug. The beer was for granddad Jones, Mr Mason, Mrs Phoebe Price or any other pensioner who would pay the price of a halfpenny.

For mum and dad, 'old ale' was boiled in an old battered saucepan on the open fire. Sometimes ginger was added but if we couldn't afford the ginger, the poker was placed in the coal fire until red-hot, and put into the ale. The family drank the mixture for colds and flu.

In the evenings, after errands – no homework from school for us poor kids from Quinton, as only jobs in local factories in Blackheath or Halesowen were expected for us if we were lucky – were knitting or corking using a cotton reel which father had hammered in four small nails. We would make a long string to tie our plaits back and would ask the local farmer for a hessian sack to peg, that is pull, pieces of cloth through the holes to form a rug. It would really help to keep the bath water warm or to place on the floor over the red stone quarry tiles, or if you were lucky, to place by the side of your bed instead of the cold floorboards.

Miss Gladys Jones

The no. 9 bus in
1916.

The cottage in Spies
Lane, dated around
1930, was situated
opposite the Black
Boy public house.

Charlotte Masters in 1940 with her Dutch girl hairstyle.

To the 'Black Boy'

The well for the house was 4 yards from the back door. When it ran dry, we walked up Spies Lane to the Black Boy, which was on the other side of the road and had an open well. Mom lowered the bucket on the rope and wound the rope back up; the bucket is full of water but also has a good chance of containing a dead animal. You then took the water home to boil on the open fire for vegetables or tea.

Albert Porter pushed his handcart with two milk churns to Bearwood seven days a week to keep his customers with regular supplies.

Miss Gladys Jones

School preparations

I began my education in September 1940 close to the first anniversary of the war, at the village school in Quinton. There were no school uniforms for infant and junior schoolchildren − only grammar school pupils had uniforms. In August my mother took me to buy all my school clothes in the village.

Firstly we visited the Municipal Bank close to the corner of College Road to withdraw the cash to pay for the clothes. The bank was always quiet and dark. Our footsteps echoed on the shiny floor and we spoke in whispers. A short walk then took us to Miss Parkes' drapers shop. There mother purchased white cotton vests with little sleeves, a set of navy blue knickers which had pockets in them to hold a handkerchief, pairs of socks and stockings and two liberty bodices. Liberty bodices were quilted, fleece-lined, sleeveless over-vests with vertical stripes of ribbon and heavy machine stitching. Suspenders were sewn on the bottom hems of the liberty bodices to hold up the black woollen stockings that we wore in winter. Houses and schools were cold then when winter arrived.

Next we walked down College Road and crossed over to the row of shops that fronted on to the Hagley Road West almost opposite the Danilo picture house. There used to be a shop there called Wanstalls. Wanstalls sold high-quality baby wear, children's clothes and lady's blouses and jumpers. One could see most of the stock through the gleaming glass fronts of the drawers that lined the walls. Mother purchased a red tartan kilt for me. It was secured at the front by a large, fancy silver pin. Next she chose a matching red blouse and a red pickwear jumper which was trimmed across each shoulder with silver buttons decorated with an enamelled red stripe. Lastly a dark navy blue topcoat was purchased.

We left Wanstalls and walked to the hairdresser's shop in High Street. Here my whiteblond hair was cut and styled into the fashionable Dutch girl cut. It was the haircut that Christopher Robin has in the *Winnie the Pooh* books, though his would have been called the Dutch boy cut.

Charlotte Tate (*née* Masters)

two
Family Life

I loved dog biscuits

The opening opposite 45 Frederick Road led you to Hagley Road; on the right was the bakery called Dewcross. It's still there now, but in olden days they did their own baking. They had hooks on the walls and they would hoist the bag up to the open window at the top.

On the left was Fletchers, the grocery shop. They wore long white aprons. In the shop were the sides of bacon hanging around with the flies. On the other side of the shop were boxes and packets of dog biscuits, cheeses in nets, butter etc. – everything you could wish for.

I would take the order in from mother for him to put up; it's a beauty shop now. I was always a queer child and I had a taste for dog biscuits so I would sit on the sacks and put my hands behind my back and get a handful of these biscuits to eat later.

Mrs Eileen Lee (*née* Clark)

The Bourne family home

Mr Swaine-Bourne worked for Chance Brothers until 1867, when he went into business on his own. He was a specialist leaded-light designer and manufacturer.

He built the chapel at the Bearwood Gospel Hall, opposite Ethel Street, which opened in 1896. Kenneth Swaine-Bourne followed in the business and lived at The Poplars, in Ridgacre Road in Quinton.

I have a photograph of Swaine-Bourne in his car taken outside Elford House in Hagley Road in Edgbaston in the 1900s. The photograph also shows Kenneth Swaine-Bourne as a young man stood in front of his motorcycle.

Brian Gastinger

A nearby piano teacher

My mother was keen for me to have piano lessons so at seven years old I was taken to Mrs Pullen, who lived at Woodgate, for instruction whilst my mother and grandma visited Aunt Florrie.

We went by the no. 208 bus, a single-decker Midland Red that went down Spies Lane and Carters Lane, terminating at Woodgate just past Carters Lane Church. They only ran about once an hour. Spies Lane in those days was only a lane with hedges and overhanging trees on both sides – very different from how we know it today. After a time, another piano teacher nearer home was found; this was Miss Vera Bourne.

The Misses Bourne lived in a big house on the corner of Ridgacre Road and Highfield Lane. It was a detached house surrounded by a garden with hedges around and a neat paved path to the big wooden porch and door.

I was in awe of this lady who seemed rather stern but who I'm sure was very nice really. It all appeared very grand in this big house though I only remember going into the drawing room where the piano stood. Looking back now, there seemed to be a lot of spinsters around – of course I realised as an adult that this was because so many young men were killed in the Great War that there simply weren't enough men to go around.

Vivienne Harris (*née* Jacomb)

Above Kenneth Swaine-Bourne standing in front of his motorcycle outside Elford House in the early 1900s; his father is seated in the car.

Below Mr and Mrs Kenneth Swaine-Bourne in the paddock of The Poplars in Highfield Lane.

Bill was in the Navy

Mom and Dad sold their shop and moved to Beech Avenue in Quinton in July 1939, then the war started in September. By that time I worked in the typist pool at Wrights Ropes in Garrison Lane. It was a terrible journey; I went to town on the no. 9 bus, walked down to Albert Street by the Beehive, then caught a tram to Garrison Lane – the fare was a white ticket, 4½d.

All the houses were there then, and young families – my mum's sister lived in Castle Road West.

There were only two shops open at the Hollybush before the war, Boots and a grocery shop. Shops at the top of White Road were Haynes the newsagents, Regal library, a dress shop, Newman's the opticians and Pramland. Opposite was Dalloways, the fish shop, and next door to that was Oglesby's the jewellers, then a furniture shop, then a big gap of waste

land where you could cut through to Beech Avenue. Suzanne's was on the corner then.

Things have changed, especially the Hollybush shops. I would take my list in on a Tuesday and on a Thursday to the Maypole; they would deliver it free of charge. Personal service has disappeared; you got to know people but now when you go into supermarkets you're just a person. On a Saturday, you could go down the Hollybush and spend an hour or more there because of all the people you would meet.

I got married in 1948. We lived with mom and dad because Bill was in the Navy and we couldn't afford to buy a house. Bill left the Navy after fifteen years' service and got £100. We used this to buy a dining table with four chairs and two fireside chairs.

We found the flat in Highfield Road where I still live. When we moved in, the rent was around 30s a week and because Bill was in the navy, I got 5s off that. His allowance was £5 per week. It was hard going but everyone was in the same boat, and nobody had a lot of money to spend. A visit to the pictures was a real treat and no one went for meals in those days, we just walked to Clent with the kids and took a picnic.

Irene Devereux

Blundetts' goodies

My maiden name was Green. My parents moved to Quinton in 1920 when I was two years old. My father was an engineer by trade.

Our cottage backed onto the top of Higgins Lane but the address was Ridgacre Lane. Next to us was Ivy House Farm, run by Charlie Clay. Up the side of Ridgacre Lane was Tom Merris, who had a dairy at the Hollybush; my father worked for him. This dairy served parts of Quinton and Blackheath for many years.

W. Merris's father owned Top Farm; further along towards Four Dwellings was another farm owned by the Burchells. The road opposite Merris's farm led to Stoney Lane and then to Hagley Road.

In the road opposite our cottage was another cottage owned by the Croft sisters and opposite there was another farm and this road led to the Hollybush; close to here was a shop called Blundetts, which sold all sorts of goodies.

The Harrises are mentioned in a book I have. They had a farm by the Kings Highway. In fact I believe they did not own the farm but in fact rented it from the Foleys.

I also remember the name W. Mullett, who served in the RAF and was awarded the DSO for bravery.

Mrs Winifred Eccles

Bed-warming bricks

I was born in 1925 in one of three cottages between the Red Lion and Hollybush public houses. My family moved to 221 Spies Lane in 1927, another cottage with two bedrooms, a living room and a kitchen.

In this cottage we had a coalhole in the corner of the kitchen and a larder with large red tiles, waist high. This was called the cold slab to keep food cool; it was also somewhere to place the home-made nettle pop to ferment. This was made with nettles, dandelion and herbs from the local hedgerows.

At 223 Spies Lane lived a nailer, Sam Price, who worked behind the two cottages. He made many articles for the locality but mainly nails, ironwork and repaired, reground and set lawnmowers. I used to pump the fire, feed the coke fire and fetch the water to cool the hot iron. My wages for the week were ½d or 1d.

When Sam Price was sixty-five he built a windmill, giving the two cottages electric light. Sam worked at Prices in Halesowen during the 1939 war. The Guests lived next door, then the Masons – Minnie, Doris, Amy,

Phoebe Price and Florence Jones sitting in the field to the rear of Sam Price's cottage in Spies Lane in the 1930s.

Renie and Sam – then Betty and Albert Porter, then the Vaughans and Hacketts.

At home during the winter, building bricks were placed in the oven of the cast-iron black leaded grate and, with the oven plate, would warm our beds. Mum and Dad had a warming pan that was filled with the cinders from the fire; it was then pushed forward and backward inside their bed.

Miss Gladys Jones

The grocery order outing

From my childhood, I remember my grandmother Lily Parish sitting in our house with her notebook making out her grocery order to take to the shop. The heavier goods were packed in a box and delivered to your door by the grocery boy on his bicycle; only the lighter essential goods were carried home.

It was a regular outing on a certain day each week to take the order to the shop. I remember going first to the bacon counter to be served and then along to the dry goods counter and so on. I watched fascinated as the money was put into a small metal container with the ticket showing the cost and, most importantly, your Co-op number. The container was attached to wires overhead; by pulling a cord it was whisked away to the cash desk where the cashier sat. The change and your ticket was placed back in the container and returned along the wires to the assistant serving you. As well as grocery, there was the Co-op milkman and breadman. During the war years, the vans were pulled by horses; it was a real treat to hitch a ride on the van.

Mrs Vivienne Harris (*née* Jacomb)

A £1 deposit

My mother and father put down a deposit of £1 on a house in Ridgacre Road after sheltering in the show house during a snowstorm on Good Friday, 26 March 1937.

The cost of the house at that time was £420. The repayments, including mortgage, rates and ground rent, amounted to around 18s a week. My father worked two evenings a week, as a relief telephone operator at the telephone house in Lionel Street, to earn the difference between the existing rent of about 11s and the repayment on the new house.

Before moving in, my mother used to walk over to the house with a friend to scrub the floors, and I was left in the front room in my pushchair. The carpenter, who was still working on the house, used to give me rolls of wood shavings which I would make into funnels.

When we moved in we discovered, in the back garden, the path to World's End Farm, which stood on the corner of World's End Lane and Ridgacre Road. In fact it was the present site of the Quinton Evangelical Free Church.

Opposite the house was an open field with a stream running through. Many happy hours were spent playing in the field and fishing in the stream. I remember that, before the stream was culverted, during heavy rainstorms it would flood over Ridgacre Road.

Bryan Palser

Gran was marvellous

Gran was marvellous with what she did. She used to come home from work and decide the bedroom needed decorating, so she popped in this wallpaper shop called Greens, got the necessary, went home, stripped the walls, did the painting, papered the walls, cleaned up and put clean curtains up. All after she had been to work.

Brian Lee

Herbs for each complaint

The 1930s were hard times. The dole queues meant no jobs for married women, and although my mum could read and write, she was only able to get cleaning jobs at the big houses. My mother used to clean one large house near the bottom of Perry Hill Road; she would earn half a crown for cleaning the whole house. The men also suffered – no work and no state benefit at that time. They would take any sort of work, odd jobs, gardening, labouring, just to earn a few shillings to put food on the table. My mum later worked for Dr Mather who was an ex-naval doctor. He had been deeply affected by his wartime escapades, being involved in the treatment of Japanese prisoners of war. However, being treated by the doctor at 1d a week was a luxury, so we were rarely at the house with the square chimneys. We would have to be cured with good old home-made remedies – herbs picked from the hedgerows and fields around our cottage, boiled in water in the old beer saucepan, and then administered regularly. There were different herbs for each complaint, then you were made to lie on the sofa covered by an old blanket with a vinegar rag on your head; 'kill or cure' as our good friend Mrs Phoebe Price would say. Oh! Happy days.

Miss Gladys Jones

Letter from the council

In 1936 we lived in Frederick Road. Father got very irate when we received a letter from the council saying that in future we would be Frederick Road in Oldbury and not Frederick Road in Quinton.

Gladys Jones, Harold 'Darkie' Edwards and Peggy Oliver sitting in the front garden of Dr Mather's surgery in Spies Lane in 1947, with the old pump behind. The house was known as Square Chimneys.

He wrote a letter to the council saying, 'You can call it what you like but as far as I am concerned I still live in Quinton. I do not live in Oldbury!'

My father felt that Oldbury was where the factories were and he wasn't living at an address where all of the factories were. They wrote to him to tell him that the front of the house was in Birmingham and the back of the house was in Oldbury.

Brian Lee

Life in the 1900s

I was born on 26 November 1899 when Churchill was a young man. Queen Victoria died when I was two years old. I've memories of days when the simple everyday things were to bring the good out of life and people were grateful for any kindness shown to each other.

I was three when I went to school. I remember it well because I had a farthing given to me for being a good girl so I bought a lucky bag.

We had slates and pencils, and fine silver sand to make pictures. We had a lovely miniature pewter tea set that belonged to one of the teachers. On Fridays we played with it and had real tea, milk and sugar. Also, the teacher bought in a bag of farthing buns. I think they are still made at one shop in Birmingham but not at that price. The years passed and as we got older we moved up to the larger class. We were a happy crowd on the whole but in those days it was two classes: rich or poor.

Manners were different; you respected each other and worked very hard. Shops were open from 6.30 in the morning till 9.00 or 10.00 at night. The coffee shops opened at 5.30 in the morning for the work people such as tram drivers, nightwatchmen, policemen and firemen. There were no canteens then; they did not appear till 1914. The coffee shop and the cook house were a godsend to the working class. The menus had good, cheap, wholesome, plain food. You could get roast beef or pork or stew with dumplings, or cottage pie or sausage and mash. The sweets were spotted dick, treacle sponge, and rice pudding or bread pudding. The dinners were 4d and the puddings 2d. Tea or cocoa was 1d and pop was ½d, coffee was too expensive. Fish shops had fish 'n' chips at 4d; you could also buy faggots, tripe and mushy peas.

Mrs Helen Cooper

The Co-op committee

As a child growing up in those difficult years of the Second World War, I became aware of my mother's involvement in the Co-op movement. The guild was not to be missed whatever else happened; it seemed to me at the time to be the highlight of mother's week. I later learnt that my grandmother, Lily Parish, her sister, Florrie Hipkiss, and Mrs Maud Parkes had been the instigators of forming the Quinton branch of the guild. I do not remember what went on at those afternoons in the parish hall but, after school was over, I used to wait by the gates until the meeting was declared at an end and the anthem had been sung. Suffice to say, I do remember the social occasions when members did a turn, the choir sang, there were solos too, and the monologues, which at the time were hard for me to understand – but later on I came to appreciate their clever wit

and humour; Mrs Moulick was expert at delivering these.

As time went by, mother – Dorothy Jacomb but known as Gwen – duly took her turn on the committee and I was schooled in how to conduct a meeting: the composition of a committee and the democratic election of officers, the importance of an agenda and so on.

Nominations were put forward by members for someone to represent them on the Halesowen and Hasbury main body committee. Mother's name was put forward. I remember the divi slips that were produced, quarterly I think, to tell each member how much she had spent. Also on the divi forms was a voting slip attached, when elections were due. We canvassed around neighbours and friends asking them for their vote and before we knew it, mother was on the committee – a sub section, the education committee. Soon after that she started to attend conferences, usually at Easter time, in places like Scarborough, Blackpool and Glasgow, leaving me, at the tender age of ten or eleven, to look after Dad and the house while she was away.

Mrs Vivienne Harris (née Jacomb)

Mother's famous wine

My family used to live in a cottage near Lower Ridgacre Farm. It was alongside this farm and on the side of Higgins Lane; our front overlooked fields. We had a pump in the garden that we used for drinking water.

Mother found she had a little free time on her hands so she took to making wine. We used to own a lovely dog and one cold winter's evening, we heard a knock on the door. When we opened it there stood the local bobby on foot patrol. He enquired as to whether or not we had a licence for our dog. He was invited in and asked if he would partake of a glass of mulled wine on such a cold night.

The Women's Co-operative Movement, c. 1940.

He came in and drank the wine while examining the licence. Well, my mother's wine became very famous in the area and you can imagine our dog licence became the most viewed one in Quinton.

Our family was teetotal but anyone was welcome to a glass of mother's mulled wine.

Mrs Winifred Eccles

Quinton, the country

I was born on 28 March 1922 and lived with mother in Frederick Road but later moved with my husband Ken to Hall Green. It was impossible during the war to get anywhere to live in Quinton, so we moved to Moseley and then to Hall Green. The war ended and Ken came home so we moved back to Quinton in Quinton Road West in 1948; the cost of the house at that time was about £2,000. There were some houses there but nothing across the road where the police station is now. In fact, the kids used to play in the fields and you could walk across there right over to Bartley Green. Gradually they filled the houses in. Opposite where Four Dwellings School is now was Four Dwellings Farm, which became derelict. The only farm we were familiar with was Beckett's Farm, which was situated where St Boniface was – if you go past St Boniface to the island and turn right, that was where Beckett's Farm was.

People wouldn't believe how country Quinton was. My father, born 1876 in Warwickshire, was a wheelwright. I think we moved to Quinton because it was country and what he was used to.

Mrs Eileen Lee (née Clark)

Quinton Road West in the 1950s.

Bath time

Friday night was always bath night. The boiler in the kitchen was stoked up with slack (very small pieces of coal, mostly coal dust). If it was a windy night, the slack would heat the water. However, if it was a calm night the boiler would not pull and so would not heat the water. Your bath was cold, with just the occasional kettle of boiling water from the open cast-iron fire grate. The bath was placed in front of the fire, all us – children first then Mum and Dad – in the same water. While you were sat in the bath, Mum would come round with the syrup of figs and a large spoon. Then dry off and on with your vest, put your one and only coat on, no dressing gowns for us in those days. At the end of the night, the old tin bath was suspended on the outside brick wall on a very large nail until next week. This took the whole evening and then to bed.

Miss Gladys Jones

Close friends

I remember Quinton in the early 1900s – the church and entrance to the school, the post office kept by Mr and Mrs Deeley, then a house. The Deeley's had two sons who went to the school.

The headmaster was Mr Burns; he was very strict and always used a long cane to punish the naughty children.

A plot of land was used by Mr Fletcher to grow vegetables and flowers. He also had a shed there and kept chickens for eggs and for eating. Next were four houses to the top of High Street.

Opposite this was the Quinton footballers' playing field; we always held our Sunday school treat there, having races, and a swing was put up on a tall tree.

In High Street there were three houses on the left-hand side going down. I was born at 8 High Street. My aunt owned all three houses. We paid around 10s a week in rent.

My best friend, Gwen Parish, lived below us in High Street. She was four years old when I first knew her and we have been friends ever since. In our young days we played games in the street such as kick the can, marbles and blind man's bluff. There was hardly any traffic so we always felt safe; we had a wonderfully happy time. Later on in the street, one or two shops opened – one sold cooked meats, then there was a fish and chip shop owned by Philip Hill and his wife.

On the other side of the street was a butcher's shop. On the corner of Bissell Street was the outdoor, from where you could fetch half a pint of beer in a jug. My mother used to have half a pint at night and in the winter used put a hot poker in to mull it.

The rest of the street was houses; Mrs Glass owned quite a few. Every Monday, always at nine o'clock, she would collect her rents.

Mr Guest, a very little man, was the village postman.

Mrs Susie Coxall (*née* Rose)

Parish hall parties

The parish hall provided me with an important step in growing up. The hall, just like the other church halls in Quinton, was available for hire for private functions, but the provision of alcohol was expressly forbidden. On one occasion I was dating a young lady who had an elder sister who was about to celebrate her twenty-first birthday at the parish hall. As the current boyfriend, I was invited to attend but by the time of the party the romance had run its course and no way was I going to this party.

My peer group, however, decided that it was only right and proper for me to honour

Dorothy and Ronald Kenning outside their butcher's shop at 15 High Street in the 1950s.

A 1953 Coronation party at the College Road Methodist church.

my obligation and attend. The pressure I was put under was quite intense, so I went.

At this time of my life I felt a little superior, having just left school and started work as a bank clerk. Friends escorted me to the party where the elder sister gave me a warm welcome. I was immediately asked what would I like to drink? – alcohol had been smuggled in.

Apart from a Christmas treat of a small glass of cider which my father allowed me, I had never drunk alcohol. Here I was, an adult, who worked for a living, being placed in a position I had no idea how to handle – how embarrassing.

Arrogance came to the rescue; the only drink I was familiar with was gin because my parents drank it occasionally: 'A gin please,' I replied. 'Fine, Keith,' was the reply.

'With orange, lime or tonic?' Suddenly I was caught and arrogance prevailed again. 'Oh! Neat please.' It was an expression I had heard at the cinema. All night I was drinking neat gin. It was awful but I wasn't going to spoil my new adult image.

At about 11 p.m. I left to go home; it was November and it was cold outside. The cold air hit me and I thought the end of the world had arrived. Was I ill? I thought I was about to die. Thank goodness there was a solid wall nearby, behind which I sought sanctuary. I stayed there for about an hour and then with a swimming head made my way home to a comfortable bed – how, I don't know. Next day my head felt as though it had been put in a vice. I had my first hangover. To this day I have not been able to acquire a taste for gin.

Keith McDonald

Full of farms

Three generations of Clays lived at Ivy House Farm at the top of Stoney Lane in Quinton. Granddad Clay used to preach at Charlie Harris's farm where Jack Cotton's offices were on the corner of Hagley Road West and the Kingsway. Later, they moved out to Hagley opposite the Gypsy's Tent. Clays used to plough the fields and carry out the haymaking.

Granddad Clay died about four weeks before I was born and they told them just after that they were going to take the farm off them. The farm was demolished about four years after Granddad died, in about 1927, to widen the road. The road altered again, when they made it a dual carriageway and then it widened again when the motorway came through. I believe the farm was owned by Lyttletons, just like the one at the top of Mucklow Hill and another down the Manor. There were about four, five or maybe six farms on the other side of the main road on the Oldbury side. There was Potter's, Hayden's, Harris's and Tinker's. Walters Road used to be Tinkers Lane.

Quinton was full of farms; there was Hagglington's by the dwellings and Merris's, and another Clay's at Upper Meadow Road. He was a second cousin to Dad and they have moved up to Illey.

Joan Smith (née Clay)

Redhall Farm Estate

We lived on Hollybush Hill, now the area between Clive Road and White Road. Three cottages were occupied by Dearns, Mr Field (brother of the Fields who were the cabinet-makers in Meadow Road), then Miss Record and her brother. There were gardens, the old Hollybush public house, then a house occupied by Haynes who used to use the front room as a newsagents. Then came Woods the nursery and then fields all the way down to the bottom of the hill where the Hollybush is today.

At the top of White Road there were three cottages occupied by Gaunt, Clinton and Andy. The latter was where the private school was situated.

All that estate, all the way to World's End Lane, belonged to Redhall Farm and the farm was where the clinic is now in Quinton Lane, then known as Harborne Lane. There was a pathway between the Co-op dairy and the end of the shops on Hagley Road West, where you could walk straight down to World's End.

The estate was sold in 1933 when Mrs Birch died and we moved to a house owned by the Partridges where the shops are at the Hollybush. The Partridges had a factory next door where they used to grind files. In 1938, the cottage next door to us was sold and the people went to live in World's End Lane; that was when Simcox was building houses by Glyn Road. We moved out and went to live in Birch Road where we stayed for forty-two years.

Lucy Dearn

Self-build houses

I joined the Birmingham fire service and shortly after that I got married to Joyce in 1953. We lived in a fire service flat at the central fire station in Birmingham for seventeen years. I then joined a self-build housing group and I built this house. It was one of seven in the group. Almost all of the houses on the estate were self-build. It died down later because of the cost of land and less ground became available. We started in 1971, finished in 1973, in fact almost two years to the day it took us to build these seven houses.

This one cost £3,900. I've since had a porch put on which cost £4,000. The Chichester Drive estate, which was built by

David Charles, was finishing off. The shell was up on the house next door and the people moved in when we were halfway to completing ours. This house was the last one to be finished on the estate.

All of Chichester, Collins Close, Samuels, Jackson Way were all self-build. Clay Drive was part of the David Charles estate. We bought the land from the City of Birmingham at a cost of £950 per plot; this site was, at one time before the war, a City of Birmingham tree nursery. Before that it was part of Smith's Howley Grange Farm.

In fact, not long after we moved in, I started to dig the garden and found about 2 feet deep of clay, which had been slung over when they built the Quinton expressway. Gradually I dug down to the beautiful loam soil which was part of the tree nursery.

Farther down towards the motorway island was Elliott's sports ground; when we were building, we found the footings of their old sports pavilion.

John Birch

Shrewsbury return for 7s 6d

I was born 11 October 1911 at 45 Waterfall Lane in Old Hill, which was then in Staffordshire. Father was called Frederick Thomas Wilson; he began work in an office in 1904 as an education officer and worked until he was eighty-seven. Every so often, he helped with the census, all hand-written in a red book. He was also an ambulance driver.

Grandfather Eli Everton was a carpenter from near Belbroughton; he made me a dobbin to pull along my teddy bears. He made fences but the best thing he made was the milk cart; he made one for Mr White and another for the Quinton milkman, Mr Harris. I would help him by throwing the water on the metal tyre that went around the ring. His brother Benjamin was a blind man who was trained at Belbroughton school to make beehives. He didn't do that; instead he went outside Birmingham market and played his fiddle, pretending to be a beggar.

My grandmother, Matilda Everton, went to the Quinton National School; I have her certificate of attendance dated 1897 framed in the other room.

We got to Birmingham on the train, from Old Hill station to Snow Hill, and then walked to the market. The transport to Quinton was nothing; we had to walk from Old Hill to Quinton, then down the hill to my aunt who lived at the corner house next to Hawthorn Farm.

Transport in the early 1900s was really the train. From Old Hill station you could go to Stourbridge and could go right to Fishguard in South Wales. Old Hill station was a junction; my uncle, Everton, was a signalman at Old Hill station and there was a branch to Birmingham in Stourbridge, Halesowen and Dudley.

You could catch the eight o'clock train from Stourbridge to Barry in Wales and would be there by dinnertime. The cost was fairly reasonable – Shrewsbury return was about 7s 6d and London was about £1.

If you wanted to go to Blackheath, you would go down Waterfall Lane to the corner; a tram would come up round Perry Park Road, Holly Road, down the High Street, to the end of the High Street and stop at the Dragon Hotel. It would come back again to go back to Cradley Heath or, if you like, on to Dudley. The price of the tram from Old Hill to Blackheath was 1d.

You will find there are a lot of pubs in Blackheath because of the men who worked in the factories making nuts, bolts and rivets, and coal mining. If you had a father down at the coal mine, you would have to take your

Certificate of Merit from Quinton National School awarded to Matilda Everton in 1897.

dad's dinner – you would take his sandwiches and a flagon of cold tea.

Horace Wilson

Watery Lane

During the school summer holidays, there were no seaside trips for the Masters children, however we had wonderful times in the countryside in and around Quinton. Among the favourite family outings were the picnics taken in Watery Lane.

My grandmother, Charlotte, would take three or more of her large, crusty loaves, butter, a stoneware jar of home-made jam, one of her big fruitcakes, tea, sugar and milk. She would fill clean, empty bottles with water.

Next she assembled her kettle, teapot, matches, newspaper, a big blanket, a tablecloth, cups, cutlery, a bat and a ball, and pack it all carefully into the deep Edwardian pram. She would tear strips from an old pillowcase or sheet to use as bandages in case any of the children hurt themselves paddling in the brook; these too were packed into the big pram.

The family would leave the house and walk down Bissell Street along Ridgacre Lane and Meadow Road past the willow trees and the pond and down the field paths to Watery Lane.

The area then was a patchwork of wild flower-filled hay meadows, cornfields and animal pasture. The field paths led to a grassy area beside a broad, shallow stream.

Clementine and Doris Masters and 'Tuppence' the horse in the Quinton countryside.

We children paddled, ran races, played tick and hide-and-seek until we were exhausted, hungry and thirsty. Never were a meal and a drink of tea so enjoyed as they were on those picnics. Afterwards we sang and told stories around the fire.

When it was time to go home, everything would be packed away into the pram.

Mrs Charlotte Tate (*née* Masters)

Small community

My father, Herbert Charles, was born on 21 November 1898 in the village of Hatton in Warwickshire. The family moved to Quinton around 100 years ago when my father was three. The family lived in one of three or four cottages situated opposite, where I believe the Studio restaurant is now. This building, owned by Harry Yeomans who was in his nineties when he died, was then a shop selling most goods. Miss Cooper ran the shop at one time.

Harry Yeomans' father, who worked at local farms as a shepherd, died when he was quite young. One of the local farms was run by a Mr Lenton, who sold his own cattle meat from his shop on the corner of Birch Road and Hagley Road West opposite White Road;

the premises are still there today at 296 Hagley Road West.

As a boy, my father worked at this butchers; he delivered on foot, carrying a basket of meat from the shop through the fields up to Warley House, which I believe he said was by the water tower in Castle Road East. He, his brothers and sisters attended Quinton Church of England School. Ernest Charles, his brother, was killed in 1916, somewhere in France. His name appears on the memorial plaque in the church commemorating all those who gave their lives in the First World War. Also his mother and sister are buried in the cemetery at the church. I have a medal awarded to my aunt, Winifred Charles, for unbroken school attendance from 1905 to 1906 at the Quinton National School.

Early in the 1800s lived two sisters, Emma and Phoebe Detheridge. Emma was a spinster and became a bit of a recluse somewhere in Romsley, I believe. However, Phoebe married William Higgins, a local lad, and they had several children. The family lived down Narrow Lane and off to the right, near to a chapel. My grandfather was a carpenter by trade; he also did the local funerals and made the coffins. I suppose they were quite well off at the time because they owned a governess horse and carriage to take them to Clent for a day's outing. They grew their own produce and kept pigs. The Higgins family farmed in Quinton at Ridgacre (pronounced Ridgicker) Farm. They also had a shop, which was licensed to sell tobacco in the name of William Higgins. Next to Four Dwellings School, at the infants' end, was a drive that led to Dwellings Farm, the home of the Clay family. One of the sons, Charlie, married my great-aunt Emma Higgins. They lived in a cottage down the hill; the cottage was situated on the corner of Upper Meadow Road. For many years a tree stood outside the cottage

Ernest Charles, who was killed during
the First World War.

and could be seen in the front gardens of the houses. I believe this is why Higgins Lane and Clay Drive were so named.

Mrs Sheila Joyner

Tiddlers in washing water

The Leasowes was our playtime favourite for all seasons – a spot of fishing using a branch from a tree with an old piece of curtain net attached with a piece of rusty old wire. We would use a jam jar for the tiddlers but only temporarily because you would get 6d for a dozen empty jam jars returned to the corner shop. We would keep the tiddlers in Mom's water butt and be later chastised for putting these dirty fish in her washing water.

We learnt to swim in the canal at the Mucklows or the Lady Pool in Manor Lane. We climbed the trees and swung on the branches, then saw how far we could climb along a tree branch without falling off. We would run past the dark half-hour pool, whispering, 'The bodies are arising from the pool'.

The Leasowes in Shenstone Valley Road – in winter sliding down the hills on an old piece of wood or rolling each other in the snow, or a spot of snowballing.

Miss Gladys Jones

George Dugmore on his motorbike at the rear of Rose Cottage at 16 Bissell Street in the late 1930s.

Jesse Rudge's general stores

When we moved here to 25 Bissell Street in 1956, Mrs Dugmore still had a little workshop in her back garden. Just above our house was Charlie's Wood Yard. He made up bundles of firewood from presumably reclaimed wood; next to that was Jesse Rudge's little general stores. He and his wife ran this shop for many years, finally closing in the 1980s when they became too old to carry on. We missed this shop very much, as it was useful to pop in for many a forgotten item and have a chat with the neighbours.

It has now been converted to a house, like many others in the village, as one by one the shops have disappeared. Such a shame, but then, that's progress we're told.

Vivienne Harris (*née* Jacomb)

three
People and Places

Hagge Farm by Apsley House

I was born in Waterfall Lane in Old Hill. The waterfall was at the back of the house. The road was very steep and it was difficult to push a pram up the hill. I would walk with Mother up Waterfall Lane, down Beeches Road, turn up Long Lane, get to the top by the Stag and walk along the Hagley Road, past the farm and the house was on the corner. I would count the cars that passed us on the way, usually about half a dozen. Up Narrow Lane, there was a factory that made bullets for the war. Behind the factory was a range where they would try the bullets out; some years later it changed over to where they made the polished steel. Opposite that was Mucklows, an iron works, then next to that was Thatcher's farm. The Mucklow family lived at the corner house which is still there.

You would go up Narrow Lane to the corner where there was a house which was a convalescent home owned by Chances, and then there was a little cottage, then the cemetery. My mother worked in the cottage off Narrow Lane as a home help.

You would walk along; there were two houses together with a big tree outside, right by the edge of the cemetery, then Hagge Farm. Where the Danilo was, used to be Danks' farm with the big house, Apsley House.

After that was Monckton House and on the opposite corner was this old barn which was Mr Harris' farm; he supplied milk to Quinton and all around. He would take the milk around; his wife used to wear a black necklace around her neck and he would say, 'What do you want, half-pint, pint or quart?'

Horace Wilson

Alford's the Newsagent

On the other side of the Hagley Road West, opposite the service road, were the two shops Alford's and Don Smith.

Alford's was the local newsagent, tobacconist, stationer and bookshop. It was also the local travel agent where you could buy train tickets for anywhere in the UK and also could book trips for the local tour company known as the Midland Red. Indeed, there were boards placed outside the shop giving details of trips to such far off places as Rhyl and Weston-super-Mare.

In my younger days Alford's provided many services for me; every Friday on my way to school I would collect my weekly journal, the *Eagle* comic, which would receive my undivided attention on the bus journey to Five Ways, which would take twenty minutes in the rush hour. As I grew older, my interest in Dan Dare and others declined and more mature weekly magazines such as *Cycling* replaced the *Eagle*. Alford's reserved my copy every week for the princely sum of 6d.

Unfortunately, in our early teens, most of us were introduced into the habit of smoking. On a very limited amount of pocket money, cigarettes were very expensive. However, at Alford's, you could buy five Woodbines for 9d and a book of matches for 1d. On a Friday night or Saturday afternoon, depending on your social arrangements, you bought your

Wellavize and W.G. Alford, shops on the corner of Hagley Road West and Walters Road.

cigarettes from Alford's before taking the escape route on a no. 9 bus to the bright lights outside Quinton, such as the Warley Odeon cinema or the ice rink at the Sandpits.

Alford's reflected the improvement in the economic climate by being one of the first shops to sell ice-cream in Quinton; I believe you had a choice of three varieties, cornet, wafer or if you were lucky a choc-ice, all made by Midland Counties Dairy. When sweet rationing ended, I bought my first packet of sweets, a tube of Rowntrees Fruit Gums from Alford's, priced 3d.

When Bonfire Night was celebrated, all the necessary fireworks could be bought from...

'Yes – Alford's!'

Every year, without fail, there would be a display case protected by a glass top. In those days, you could buy penny bangers, canon bangers and jumping jacks without any trouble. The only problem came when adventurous young boys tried to finish the task Guy Fawkes set out to do.

Mr Alford lived in a house next door to the shop. I always recall as a lad thinking 'how nice it must be only having a few yards to walk to work each day'.

Keith McDonald

Almost had a fit

A policeman called Mr Wiggins lived in the house at the corner of Hagley Road and High Street. One day I nearly had a fit when I went to call for his daughter; he was there washing and he was as bald as anything. He must have worn a sandy coloured wig but you didn't notice that under his helmet so I was shocked when I saw him bald.

Mary Davis (*née* Watson)

Church recollections

Among the regular members of the Primitive Methodist church were members of the Bissell family. Mrs C.W. Rose, who gave the birthday cake for the Jubilee celebrations in 1938, and her family, were also regular worshippers there. I recall the Revd John Anderton was the minister from 1918 until 1925 and

Christ Church Sunday school in the rectory grounds, 1907.

throughout that time he lived in the manse with his family, which included his daughter Joan who was about my own age.

Mr Ewart Reed, whom many Langley people will remember as headmaster of Titford Road boys' school for many years, was educated at Bourne College. I knew Mr Reed and his wife well; her parents were Mr and Mrs J. Parkes who attended the Wesleyan chapel as I did.

Some good concerts were put on at the present Methodist church. I remember that some of my friends who attended Quinton parish church were allowed to take part in the chorus.

Each year, when the garden party was held at the parish church vicarage, the children from the Church of England day school performed country dances and there was a may-pole on the rector's lawn. The Revd W.A. Rowlands and the Revd L. Palmer were rectors at that time.

QLHS Archive

Architect in Quinton

In December 1959, at the age of thirty-seven, I decided to commence my own architectural practice in the old Monkton farmhouse and barn in Quinton, located at the corner of the Kingsway and Hagley Road West. The offices were vacated by Messrs Keight, the solicitors, who decided to practise from premises near to the Stag and Three Horseshoes. Stone, Hooper and Pickard occupied the single-storey part of the building. A building contractor, Mr Rowe, remained in part of the cottage for a brief period after I moved in.

Owing to the very poor structural condition of this two-storey building, it was not practical to use the first floor area at all, but by fitting curtains to the upper windows, it gave a more habitable appearance.

Within a few months, my practice flourished and the small cottage rapidly filled with assistants. Warning signs that the building was unsafe came when a heavy roof timber crashed through the ceiling into the ground-floor office. Fortunately, no one was injured but this prompted the owner, Rex Houghton, to embark upon a redevelopment of the site in 1960.

Stone, Hooper and Pickard required the ground-floor offices and I opted for the first-floor area, leaving the second floor available for letting as offices. Stone, Hooper and Pickard later changed their name to Jack Cotton.

One of the first occupants of the second-floor offices was Sarah Coventry who was engaged in the assembly and distribution of costume jewellery around the country. After a few years, the Midlands Electricity Board took over the second-floor tenancy where they remained in occupation until well after my retirement in September 1989.

In addition to Stone, Hooper and Pickard, the ground-floor accommodation comprised three self-contained shops. Norsk Design, a Norwegian shop selling quality gifts; Don Smith, a grocer; and a ladies' hairdresser, Sylvia, were the first occupants of the shops.

Derek J. Smart

Commercial tidings

At the back of the old churchyard was a bank and fields, just a lane with no houses. Down to the bottom of High Street, there was a brick wall with a hedge in front; they've widened it now. Straight opposite were four

The view from College Road towards the Kingsway in the 1950s; Shawton House is the flat-roofed building in the centre, between the lamp-post and the telegraph pole.

Parkes family wedding; the men across the centre are Jim, Harry and Ted.

cottages joined together. Alf Horton had the one on the right; he used to keep pigeons and grow white and red Michaelmas daisies, which he sold. Where the snicket is, now called The Green, there were two or three cottages there, occupied by the Baggotts and the Whyles. The three houses are still there to the left of the park entrance; Fred Clay had the house built on the end. To the left of the nailer's cottage was the New Inns and at the back of there were two other cottages.

Arnold Parkes, an engineer, bought Pax Hall from Miss Husseyfreek. Oh! He was a lad. He used to live in one of the houses where Scrivens is now, and he used to have a little building in Bissell Street, where they've built two or three new houses.

Another Parkes owned the little factory where Redman's is now; we used to take our accumulators for charging for the wireless, 4d or 6d.

In High Street was the old fish 'n' chip shop, where the takeaway now is, then a general store where the hairdresser is now. Next door, which was made into a house, was a hairdresser, Wrights. Then there was Groves, the fruiterers, at the top of High Street, on the left-hand side going down. My uncle Will Mullett helped with the fire service. My dad used to deliver the coal but I don't know who for.

Arnold Parkes had a building where the new houses are; he used to make little odd tools. He also used to regrind the rollers for Shredded Wheat in Welwyn Garden City. He also had a milk bar where the bookmakers are now. There was a row of shops there: Slims, the pet shop; a big greengrocers; West's, a newsagent; a café on the end where the road is now, and a ladies gown shop.

John Round

Shops moving on

Arnold Parkes used to own a café or milk bar right opposite the Highway, opposite Beattie Taylors, who lived in one of the cottages still there today called Highway Cottage, over the top of the motorway. The buildings from the Toll House towards Halesowen were the Wesleyan chapel, then two little cottages, then a greengrocers, Law's the barbers, Homer's the butchers, a dry cleaners, a baby linen shop, then Slim's the seed shop. The betting shop and fish bar are there now.

There were cottages where the motorway bridge is now, occupied by the Baggots and Joneses. The Danilo, built in 1939, was on the site of Apsley House, where Danks lived. The Thatchers lived in a house by the side of the Slyng, a single-track road by the side of Apsley House. Mr Thatcher was a barber who used to cut the old men's hair at Quinton Hall. Betty Whittaker had money left to her, and went to live with Phyllis Rose, Billy Rose's daughter.

Down College Road was Preece the electrical shop, next door was Winnie Thurban, a grocers, where the TV man is now. Where Scrivens now is were two old cottages, occupied by Lenna Foxall and Billy Rose. Billy repaired the petrol pumps. Of a night Billy would have a couple of drinks, put a policeman's hat on and play the accordion on the top of High Street. I also remember Nora Parkes the drapers, Parkes the ironmongers, Charlie Sorrell the butchers, and later Bridges. The first Municipal Bank round the corner

Hagley Road West, c. 1924. The shops and offices are, from left to right, Barclays Bank, Joseph Parkes Drapers and Moyle & Co.

Arthur Masters, the Quinton fireman, now retired, in the yard at the back of 17 High Street in the 1930s awaiting a regular trip to Ludlow Races.

was built by Bryants, and next door was a chemist called Mayer with an opticians on top.

On the other side of the road was Ganes the undertakers, a Co-op grocers, Mrs Jordan's cake shop – where the Midland Bank was, Pearson's drapers shop, which later became a cycle shop, Millward & Cutler – Mr Millward had a car which he ran as a taxi, then came Cutlers, a shoe shop which sold leather shoes and did repairs, then a large grass bank, then the Co-op greengrocers, then Harris's farm.

Lawrence Basterfield

Fireman Masters' Quinton move

The family came to Quinton on a snowy day in 1908. My aunt Florence, born in June of that year, was a baby-in-arms. They moved into the fireman's house in Bissell Street and began a new life there. It would be a better life for the children to live away from the city and a safer job for Arthur, now in his forties with a large family to support. When he left Birmingham he was presented with two paintings of his favourite horses, one was a grey, the other a chestnut. Their names were Franklin and Frizzel. The paintings always hung on the wall of the front room on either side of the piano.

In Ridgeacre Lane, just around the corner from their house, was the small fire station. It was a lofty, glass-fronted building, and even when I was a girl one could look through the window and see the old fire-fighting equipment inside.

It was necessary for Quinton village to maintain a modest fire station and a resident fireman, as many of the villagers were nail-makers. Their cottages were prone to catch fire because of the nature of the work they had to do. There he would put out fires in nail-makers' cottages, household chimney fires, haystack fires and suchlike. Other duties included maintenance of the fire-fighting equipment.

Other work undertaken by Fireman Masters was fire-watching for Zeppelins during the First World War.

Charlotte Tate (*née* Masters)

Their own tennis court

On the corner of Highfield Lane and Ridgacre Road are some new houses. They were built on land occupied by a garage and before the garage was built, there stood on the site a lovely house called The Poplars.

It was the home of Swaine-Bourne and his wife Dora, who lived there from the early 1900s until 1961. The family had its own tennis court and well.

Adjoining the house was a stable and pad-dock for the horse and coach.

Swaine-Bourne ran his own family business in Birmingham. The firm manufactured stained-glass windows and he is reputed to have been the first man in Birmingham to have a motor car.

The Bournes had two children, Sue and Muriel. When she grew up, Sue became a piano teacher and gave lessons at the house.

Mrs Georgina Prescott

Saturday evening bargains

The Bullring had a wonderful clock in the market hall that was completely destroyed; also the Singer Sewing Machine Co. had great big dolls, which were beautifully dressed in satin, demonstration dolls I think they were. I would go into the Bullring on a Saturday evening; they had flares on the stalls because there were no electric lights then and all the butchers and the fruit people would sell everything off cheap, bag of oranges for 1s, because there was no refrigeration in those days. There was a poultry market, a meat market and a fruit and veg market. I remember a wonderful grocers called Morrells; they had those great big can-isters with the tea and it would be called a high-class provision.

Joyce Birch

The sweet cobbler's

The last property in Frederick Road was a sweet shop and, just round the corner, was a cobbler's – both in the same house.

The cobbler's shop had wonderful smells; he cut his own leather. If you can imagine the old image of a cobbler with wire specs and an apron, that was him. But as well as that, on the side was a counter with sweets in glass jars. Just like walking into a shop at the Black

The stagecoach in the paddock of The Poplars in Highfield Road.

Country Museum, and he used to pick them out with his hands and drop them into this pointed, triangular bag. We used to have six-penarth or whatever of every conceivable sweet you could imagine. He had a gas lamp and when it got dark he would pull this wire and it got brighter. The premises sadly were demolished.

Brian Lee

Food rations

Dad always fancied owning his own business. Little did we realise that after just a few years, the Second World War would be upon us,

Advertising literature from Paynes Shoe Repairs, who had a branch in College Road.

bringing with it all sorts of problems to any people who were involved in the grocery trade.

With the outbreak of war, most foodstuffs went on ration and everyone was issued with a ration book, which entitled them to a very small amount of butter, sugar, bacon, cheese, tea, bread, eggs etc.

In these books were very small tokens, which had to be cut out by the retailers, counted and then sent off to the Ministry of Food. The local office for us was at the Borough Hall in Halesowen. Sugar used to be delivered to us in bulk along with the familiar old stiff blue paper bags into which we had to weigh the sugar and seal them up. The weights and measures inspector used to come round unannounced to check any items they chose, to verify that the weights were accurately measured out.

The scales and counter weights were also regularly checked. Butter and cheese also had to be cut up, weighed out and wrapped.

Dad used to have his bread delivered daily by Wimbush in their familiar green vans. Wimbush was a famous bakery in Green Lane in Small Heath in Birmingham (long since gone). People soon got to know when the baker was due and they used to form a queue outside the shop in order to buy what sort of bread they wanted. The bread was all in unsliced; sliced bread had not then come about.

These days we are all used to buying biscuits in small packs from the supermarkets; back in those days biscuits were always delivered to the shops in large tins to be weighed out and bagged as required. There were always some breakages, which used to be sold off cheaply.

Sweets also were weighed and bagged as required. Food rationing went on for a number of years after the war, being relaxed very gradually. Other things were also in short supply then, such as tobacco and cigarettes, but they were not rationed.

I think I was about seventeen when I started smoking but I was lucky enough to have a constant supply at hand. I was also popular at work as I used to supply some of my work mates with them. Later on, clothing also went on ration.

Clive Davies

Where we were born

I remember climbing Red Lion Hill with my sisters on our way to the Church school at the back of Quinton church.

At the back of the Red Lion was a short cul-de-sac where you could see grandfather's cottage where Father was born. There were several cottages going down the hill from the Lion, one of which my younger brothers and sisters were born in.

The Hollybush inn was halfway up the hill, then called Beech Lanes.

I remember the horse buses travelling from Bearwood to College Road in Quinton and the end of the village as it was then.

One thing that stands out in my mind was the driver of a horse bus pretending to break the paper decorations we had across the road with his whip. The decorations were for the coronation of George V and Queen Mary in about 1910.

Below Clothing coupons from 1944-45.

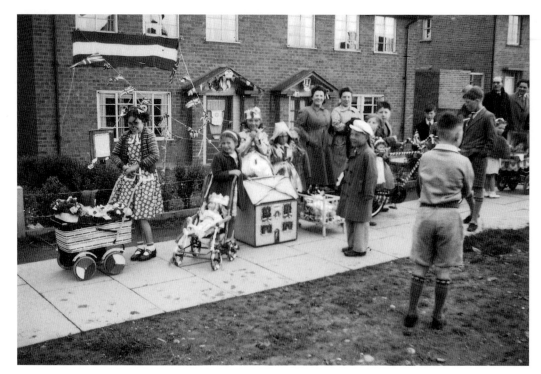

Coronation celebrations in Quinton Road West.

Farms were all over Quinton; the fields of Baker's Farm surrounded our garden. The Brennands of Brandhall used to come to church in a horse and carriage; they had a large house with a beautifully kept garden.

The picture of the Red Lion is not very old as it was much narrower in my early days. It was later widened to enable buses to pass; there was no Wolverhampton Road then and all the buses to Kidderminster, Wolverhampton, Stourbridge, Dudley and Halesowen went along there.

Mrs Elsie Hall (*née* Blundell)

Medical memories

Dr Mather at Square Chimneys had a Morrison shelter, which was a steel table with mesh down the side. Dr Mather was also a councillor for Halesowen. Another doctor was Dr Daley, who lived in Ridgacre Road; he attended the men in Quinton Hall. The staff used to put concerts and pantomimes on; Mr and Mrs Piper were the Master and Mistress, Mr Daley's wife was a dancer. Mr and Mrs Gordon were the caretakers and lived in the house on the corner. Miss Dugmore was the Quinton midwife. Later the Quinton midwife was Nurse Parkes.

Mrs Joan Smith (*née* Clay)

Dressed correctly

Next door to Mr and Mrs Rutter, in a large old house called Pax Hall, there lived Miss Hussyfreek and her brother. Miss Husseyfreek was a very well known local figure, as she played tennis on the Henry Wiggins tennis courts until she was about eighty years of age and she always dressed correctly in a white tennis dress. The house she occupied in Ridgacre Lane was demolished to make way for the feeder road to the M5 motorway.

Miss Cutler

Quinton's Methodists

I remember Tinkers Farm in Tinkers Lane and Mr Foley's farm which stood on almost the same spot as the Kings Highway Hotel now occupies; this could well have been the farmhouse where Mr Chatwin lived. Mr Chatwin fitted up an old barn at the corner of Monckton Road and Hagley Road, which was used by the Methodists for their services for about twelve years. I often went to the old farmhouse, which stood on the corner of Stoney Lane, as the grandparents of one of my friends lived there. I remember a very large old tree in their garden, this may have been the one that Mr Stringer of Cradley, who visited Quinton in 1818, conducted services under. Edwin Danks was the founder of the

Above Nurse Parkes, the Quinton midwife, with Marjorie Phillips, aged three weeks.

Below Tinkers Farm Estate in Apsley Road and the Kingsway was acquired for housing development. The builders named are S.H. Rowe and Peter Danks.

boiler-making and engineering firm, based in Oldbury.

I believe that in his earlier years he lived in Langley and then later moved to Quinton. This was quite the usual thing for our local industrialists to do in the later years of the nineteenth century, since Quinton was within easy driving distance of their works by horse and trap and yet was away from the smoke and chemical fumes of Oldbury and district.

His move to Quinton proved a boon to the local Methodists, for Mr Danks bought an area of farmland that was then under cultivation and gave it as the site for the present Methodist church in College Road. He also provided a house for the minister and in 1911 gave £400 to pay off the remaining debts on the church and on the school premises.

Mr and Mrs C.E. Rutter lived in Ridgacre Lane. Mr Rutter was very well known in the district and played a big part in the life of the Quinton Methodist church.

Indeed, he must have established something of a record, I should imagine, for he was its organist from 1896 till 1938, and although his organ 'blower' received a very small sum for his labours, Mr Rutter's services as organist were always purely voluntary. At the end of those forty-two years, the members of the church showed their appreciation of his services by presenting him with a cheque and an electric clock.

Miss Cutler

A penny and an orange

At the back of the houses in Meadow Road was Quinton Park where there was a shelter and swings and a big valley where we all went to play.

The staff and management of Quinton Hall in the 1970s.

At the other end of the Park was Howley Grange. There was a farm house where there used to be a small cottage and a nail shop. It was said that King Charles II spent time in hiding from his enemies around here. He left his spear in the barn roof and as long as it remained there, no tithe was paid for the farm.

Then there was Bourne College, hence College Road, a gentleman's school. Mr Hoosen was the headmaster; he lived there with his sister and two daughters. Every Christmas, the village children went carol singing there and they all had a penny and an orange. Now there is a housing estate where the college stood, one road named Hooson Close.

Mrs Susie Coxall (*née* Rose)

Marilyn Ditch and her brother standing in front of the shelter in Quinton Park.

The bells jingle jangle

We moved to Frederick Road and rented the house in Frederick Road for about 7s a week. In the kitchen we had a big wooden table and chairs, no fitted kitchens then.

A cold water tap, no hot water. An outside toilet with a one-holer wooden seat, no lights, just a candle and the paper we used was news-paper which had been cut up and hung from a piece of string. We were the first people in Frederick Road to have electricity in the early 1930s.

Frederick Road was a little quiet haven and we used to play out all day. I was a bit of a tomboy and I used to play Cowboys and Indians with the lads; I was always tied up to the lamppost. There was Frederick Road, which led on to Birch Road and Birch Lane. Apart from the houses in Birch Road there were no other houses up the other side; on the corner of Birch Road and Kenilworth Road there was the old outdoor that we used to call Fanny Tuffleys; she was an old lady who was always a bit aggressive. She had one of these bells on the door and when we were

kids we would push the door open, just to hear the bell jingle-jangle. I would also go there for Mrs Morris, a friend of my mum, to collect her ale in a jug; she would pay me a penny for the errand. Further on down was the big open space, which was Turner's the basket-makers. On the other side were cottages; there was a cutting through from Birch Lane to Stanley Road; it is now called Rose Avenue. There was a piece of land that Johnson took over and started putting old cars on. Johnson's took over the piece of ground and started selling milk. In Birch Lane was Baches, the milk people, where Dairy Court is now. Right at the end of Birch Road to the junction of Castle Road, the big house on the corner was where Baches lived. In Frederick Road were Wacadans, Wathes, Cattel and Gurden; they were right at the top of Frederick Road, the offices were situated where the new houses are now. I can remem-

Harwoods charabancs, whose premises were in Frederick Road, with a crowd ready for a trip to the seaside.

ber being woken up by the horses coming back off the round; they would trot up Frederick Road, turn right into Gateley Road and then turn right again into the back of the stables. Also in Frederick Road was a company called Harris's and also one called Harwoods, the Coaches. Harwoods had charabancs; he did trips to Aberystwyth, Blackpool and Rhyl.

Mrs Eileen Lee (*née* Clark)

Several Clays

Ivy House Farm was run by the Clays. Emma Clay was born Emma Higgins; she was only skin and bone. Mom used to cook her a cake because she wasn't very domesticated. The Clays were at the farm on Upper Meadow Road where they sold the milk from. Emma's husband was called Charlie and my father was Charlie Clay and they were really like blood brothers, my dad was dark but Charlie Clay at the farm was sandy haired and very freckly complexion with a heavy moustache. But

when they took the farm off Dad, I was four. It was compulsory purchase because they wanted to widen Stoney Lane and they built three lovely houses down there.

Granddad Clay had died so Dad had to seek out further employment, so he went on to the railway and worked with the horses there. They demolished those houses when they put the expressway through.

George Davis owned the house and farm up Perry Hill and we have a photograph of him with his milk cart and horse.

Mrs Joan Smith (*née* Clay)

The horse is tired

Arnold Parkes, with his wife Renie, came round the corner of Meadow Road in his horse and trap; they had both been drinking and as he turned into High Street he told his wife to 'get out cause the horse is too tired to pull the weight up High Street'.

She wouldn't get out, so he got out, unhitched the horse and guided the horse up

Horse and cart milk deliveries by G.F. Davies.

Harry Parkes behind the wheel of his car.

Philip H. Birch with his wife Winifred and their children Phillip, Marie Louise and Donald at Warley House, *c.* 1916.

High Street, only for the trap to fall backwards and his wife went sprawling on the pavement. He had a big American car and he used to drink in the Kings Highway.

Lawrence Basterfield

Steeped in local history

My personal association with Quinton began in 1916 at the age of two. Later, I moved outside the boundary of Birmingham and Oldbury.

My mother, except for a brief sojourn in Bearwood, has lived in Quinton and Warley all her life. Her mother and grandmother also spent practically all their lives in the district.

The district is steeped in local history. The older inhabitants tell many tales of horse buses, bygone personalities and so on, as well as recalling the days when Warley Hall and Lightwoods Park were private residences.

I can remember the days of fields, farms, brooks and cottages before the building development obliterated the country aspect. Of course, much of what is Quinton today was not so called in those days. Hagley Road West was known as Beech Lanes from the Kings Head to approximately Birch Road. The area round the Hollybush was The Hawthorns.

Anyone who has ever read Francis Brett Young will agree with his references to 'the debauched village of Tilton'.

H.C. Johnson

Apprenticeship

I am not sure if I qualify as a Quintonian after fifty years in exile, but here goes!

I was born at 116 Harborne Road, which I suppose was a nursing home, on the 4 April 1943, the start of Hitler's decline!

The only child of Charles Stanley Jones and Muriel Alice (*née* South), we lived at 19 Shenstone Valley Road where my parents had been since their marriage in 1939.

Father attended a school attached to Blackheath church and left when he was thirteen and a half years old for an apprenticeship in bookbinding at The Artistic Engraving and Printing Co. in Great Charles Street in Birmingham.

In fact, he stayed there for fourteen or fifteen years and it was there that he met my mother. By the mid-1930s he had taken City and Guilds qualifications in carpentry and joinery and perhaps by 1936 was working for Rudge Brothers who were building houses in Kingsway. George Rudge was a friend of father's – probably they had a shared interest in tennis and football. There was also Les Rudge with whom father ran a fruit and vegetable shop at Weoley Castle after the war.

From those early days I recall that living near us were Brian Evans, John Cherry, Norman Harris and Michael Ankorn. Also the Riley, Ferriday, Alcock, White, Waterhouse, Westwood, Barrett and Church families.

Looking back over fifty years there seem to have been a large number of shops in a small radius of where we lived. There were two at the bottom of Shenstone Valley Road of which one was a sweet shop and round the corner in Howley Grange Road was a chemist called Colclough, a newsagent whose name escapes me but he and his wife were big ballroom dancing fans. I remember going there each winter on a Saturday evening to collect father's *Sports Argus*. The couple would be dishing out these papers dressed in all their evening finery and the door was firmly bolted at 7 p.m. after which I guess they would be off to the evening's entertainment.

There were more shops at the top of Shenstone Valley Road: Wrensons the Grocer and Tonks the Butcher; there were possibly three more as well. My mother still recounts that the butcher's daughter called each morning for the meat order and it was delivered later in time for lunch. Also I think the grocer's boy called each week for the order book which Mother had written up and he delivered the supplies later in the week, returning the book and collecting the cash.

Stuart Jones

Rotten as a pear

Talking of memories of the old farms, in Halesowen in the 1930s was an old chap called Charlie Rot. He was called 'Rot' because all his teeth were as rotten as a pear. He would come up Mucklow Hill to Quinton on a Saturday morning with his horse and cart selling greengrocery and fresh fish. He parked in the farmyard at Perry Hill and people would come from all around to buy his vegetables and fish. The fish was always covered in flies.

John Birch

Horse whips were drawn

One amusing story my father told me: sometime in 1925, Grandfather was in Lightwoods Hill canvassing for new customers. Ernie Bache, his business rival, was doing the same thing. They were both in their horse-drawn floats accusing each other of being on their pitch. Horse whips were drawn and a Roman-style chariot fight ensued. They were both prosecuted for causing an affray, appearing in court at Smethwick. It was reported in the *Smethwick Telephone*.

John Birch

Fred Bissell made coffins

The wife's parents bought the house in Bissell Street in 1921; it cost £300 and today there's a house for sale up the street, a hundred and odd thousand. I think these houses were built in 1878.

A builder built this house, just a single house for himself, then he built the adjoining terrace houses for his workers. The opening was to keep the firm's building cart in and the horse was kept somewhere up the garden. I used to garage my car up the street in Hilda Lowe's garage.

Fred Bissell was a carpenter, builder and he made coffins. Someone called Masters ran the outdoor, then it was closed as a pub/outdoor in about 1970 and someone opened it up selling clothes; then it was an antique furniture shop.

Harry Cook

Inglenook Cottage

I am an old Quintonian, and I was born eighty-six years ago in the cottage to the side of the New Inns public house. The cottage is still there, albeit extremely modernised and called Inglenook Cottage. Just to the left is the entry to the cottage, which is still there today. The property was sold when the pub was knocked down to make way for the Kings Highway.

The garden was quite large and provided us with fruit and vegetables for the winter months. My father died when I was eight years old; this meant that my mother and the family had to work very hard.

I remember we had a square piece of garden full of beautiful lilies of the valley. One day the butcher came to see my mum; he suggested that we pick the lilies and put them in bunches so he could sell them for us in his shop. The

John and Agnes Masters behind the counter of the outdoors at 17-19 High Street, dated 1954.

Ernie and Margaret Willetts in the garden at Inglenook Cottage, c. 1918.

HARBORNE WARD.

MUNICIPAL ELECTION, Nov. 1st, 1926.

VOTE EARLY.   8 a.m. to 8 p.m.

VOTE for DUGMORE
The Labour Candidate.

The council election literature of James Dugmore on 23 October 1926.

work was back-breaking but worthwhile as it helped a lot with the housekeeping.

Mrs Margaret Bate

The over-burdened ratepayer

The following was written on James Dugmore's election leaflet of 23 October 1926:

I have again been approached by the Labour Party and a number of electors in the Harborne Ward to allow myself to be nominated for this election, and I may say, having regard to the fact that over 1,000 of the electorate gave me confidence by voting for me on the last occasion, I have decided to accept the pressing call.

When the re-assessment shortly to be made in the city is in progress, I suggest that our representatives on the council table take a resolution petitioning Parliament for compulsory power to rate and tax all ground values. I should strongly support any effort put forward with this in view if elected in the interest of the already over-burdened ratepayer.

I cannot believe that the great mass of the electorate of the city are in agreement with many of the laws now operating and yet they do not avail themselves of the opportunity of recording their votes when the occasion arises. If this applies to you, turn up at the poll and vote for the People's Man, who had nine years' experience on the Quinton council before being annexed by the city and is willing to give you faithful service.

James Dugmore

The Willetts family outside Inglenook Cottage in 1915. In the photograph are Albert Willetts, his wife Lizzie, seated, and other family members: Elsie, Winifred, Ernie and Margaret.

Margaret, the champion sprinter

My grandfather Albert Edward Willetts and his wife Lizzie moved into 487 Ridgacre Lane, later named Inglenook Cottage when they were married around 1890. They had eight children, two of whom died when they were babies.

Albert was a builder's labourer and Lizzie took in washing to make ends meet. The eldest daughter, Elsie, went into service in Torquay on leaving school and sent home money to help the growing family.

Robert, the eldest son, was killed in the First World War, aged twenty-one. His name is in Christ Church in Quinton on a plaque of remembrance for all those local boys who were killed in the 1914-18 War.

My father, William Ernest, was born in 1912. The second youngest, he did very well

at school and could have gone to grammar school. Unfortunately, Grandfather died when he was ten years old so he had to leave school at an early age and go out and support the family.

There was a lot to do in the cottage; my father and his youngest sister Margaret returned from school at lunch times to help with the washing, scrub the floors and clean the black lead cooking range.

They kept chickens in the garden and grew all the fruit and vegetables they ate. The ancient pump in the garden was used for all the water.

Margaret Willetts was a champion sprinter for the school team. She was fourteen years old when she competed in the All Birmingham schools sports day at Queen's

Park in Harborne. She would have joined Birchfield Harriers but funds prevented this happening until she was eighteen.

In the Second World War, a bomb went off close by in Watery Lane and Grandmother was thrown across the room of the cottage, no damage done apparently but she died a few months later.

Auntie Winnie Willetts was the last resident of the cottage. When she died in 1988, aged eighty-seven, the cottage was returned, sadly for our family, to the owners and put up for sale. It has been renovated and does look a lot different from how I remember it as a child.

Margaret is the only member of the Willetts family from the cottage alive today and she lives in North Wales.

Mrs Vivian Lawton (*née* Willetts)

Brenda the St Bernard

I lived in Quinton alongside the park in Meadow Road. Oddly enough my sister and I both have bedroom suites made from large trees that used to be at the entrance of Ivy House Farm.

When you came out of Meadow Road you would come across The Green towards the village pub, the New Inns. There used to stand a cottage and a thatched wooden cow-shed, which as children we were always scared to go past. It used to be known as Sadler's Hovel from the names of the folk who had lived there.

I remember the farm owned by William Foley and on a bank, just in front of that farm, was a general shop, which was owned by Mrs Macdonald and Miss Olivia Macdonald. Opposite the Old Toll House was another house occupied by some people named Gaunt.

I remember a very old lady named Mrs Dimmock who lived in the cottages opposite Ivy House and was an aunt of Ben Yates. Ben Yates owned a St Bernard dog called Brenda; the dog was very well known in the district.

Alongside Mrs Dimmock's cottage was a shop where Colliers sold newspapers and sweets. Next door was where the Detheridges lived. I recall old Mr Detheridge giving me 2d for saying the tongue twister 'Peter Piper picked a peck of pickled pepper'. This was when Mr Detheridge visited my father in connection with interments; I think that he must have been responsible in some way for burials in Quinton.

QLHS Archive

A children's play area

When we moved here, it was 1938. The park was started in 1901; Miss Parrish, a wealthy lady who lived at the top of Mucklow Hill bought the land for the pleasure of a children's play area. She also left Maggie Hodges, up College Road, £600–1,000 – a lot of money in those days. She was possibly Miss Parrish's housekeeper. Mr Heber Rose used to have a smallholding there and he lived in a small cottage in Meadow Road. Birmingham Parks records state that the Quinton parish council acquired for the sum of £325 from the Trustees of Mr John Darby 1¼ acres at Meadow Road with the right to use the road from Meadow Lane in common with other users.

Mrs Joan Smith (*née* Clay)

Mother Smith

Mum used to work all the hours God sent; she used to get up early for Dad and didn't go to bed until about eleven at night; she never stopped. She was an amazing person; used to make all our clothes, used to make our suits, take in other peoples washing, keep ducks. I used to hatch these ducks out in my incubator and had some marvellous results with that. She used to feed them up until just before they got their pinfeathers and then she'd feather, dress and finally sell them for a few extra bob.

With five children of her own, she would still take other people's washing in, make rugs, and make our clothes; of course she was a marvellous cook, and it's amazing what she used to do. She never stopped from when she got up in the morning to the time she went to bed at night – she never stopped. She didn't expect anything else, just used to do it. I think she enjoyed working and of course they hadn't got hot and cold water, they'd got a coal fire to cook in – an oven. We did have a gas stove later on, but we used to cook in the oven at one time.

When Mom lived in Woodgreen Road, she'd got a pendulum clock and the pendulum came off. Instead of going tick-tick-tick-tick, it went tick, tick, tick, tick much faster. I called

An invoice from William Mullett, the coal merchant, dated 1894. The invoice is made out to Quinton church for 10cwt of coke gas including carriage for 8s 6d.

to see her; she was sweating and said, 'Oh dear, oh well, I don't know what's happened to the time this morning'. I went to look at the clock; I could see what was wrong and said, 'You've got a clock that's going about ten times faster than it should do,' and she was trying to keep up with it. 'No wonder,' she was saying, 'I can't get any work done this morning!'

She'd been flying up and down the stairs and I can imagine her dashing everywhere. When I looked at the clock you could see the fingers moving and she was trying to keep up with it – amazing.

Smith Brothers Family

Mullet the coal merchant

My great granddad William Mullett was a coal merchant in Blackheath; he was married to Eliza. One of their children, George Isaac, who was born in 1879, married Amy Waldron on 6 August 1900. They had eight children and they lived in Foley's house after Miss Foley died in about 1937-38. Miss Foley kept two Pekinese.

Foley was related to the Foley's of Witley Court and rode about in a pony and trap.

The family bible presented by George Cadbury to Amy Waldron also mentions a fire in Foley's house on 11 June 1906.

John Scanlon

Old Quinton Rectory

I have wonderful memories of our lovely home for twelve years. I remember the chimney on the right which was taken away. The house was altered in so many ways. It had steps everywhere, a lovely hall through a side door in the porch, which had a fireplace, two wide steps down to the stone floor, two steps into the scullery, two steps up to the bathroom and steps up to the attic which was a little tower. I don't believe I ever went in that.

Quinton's summer festival at Christ Church rectory on 13 June 1959.

The garden was superb with vegetables at the front. There was a wonderful lime tree on the lawn. An actress from *The Archers* opened one garden fete at the rectory with over a 1,000 people attending.

The whole area was surrounded by a hedge which my husband had to cut by hand whilst talking to his parishioners.

There was the field close by where we made a tennis court by the Scout hut.

The verger and his wife, Mr and Mrs Ball, were very keen on old-time dancing, with coaching every Monday. I remember the Boxing Day dance which was a grand occasion; they did everything then.

So many people attended the church; we had to have two services in the evening. Friends wouldn't come in the morning because it was so crowded; the estates had just been built.

Edward was up and down to the cemetery on his bicycle; we didn't have a car for years.

He did thirteen weddings one Saturday, because there was some tax concession looming, every half an hour starting at 8.30 a.m. He didn't have a break to eat or drink all day.

Mrs Delia Compton

Please and thank you

I was born in July 1933 and never married. I have lived in the same house, 128 Ridgacre Lane, and never moved. Mum and Dad were walking round the area, saw the house and put a £5 deposit on it, which was a lot of money in those days.

I've seen Quinton change quite considerably over the years. I remember the shops up in Ridgacre Road, Holmes the outdoor who always made sure you said 'please' and 'thank you' to him; Walkers the newsagents; Arthur Hadley, the butcher; Lattimer the greengrocers; next was a general store that later became

Christ Church rectory grounds.

a hairdresser; next was Homesures then came Mrs Daniels at the end.

The ground opposite was all fields – no bus depot, hardly any houses around the area. Higgins Lane was just being built and today if you know all the different architecture you can see all the different building limits before they built the council houses.

The council estate opposite Higgins Lane wasn't built till the late forties, but during the war there was a great big field full of ox-eye daisies.

I cadged a job with a young lady who worked with the land army delivering the milk in the area.

Bill Deeley

The old Potters sign

I was going down Hagley Road West recently when I saw that the Sprinterprint shop was empty. Their sign had been removed and had exposed 'Potters, the butchers and greengrocers' underneath.

This must have been the wartime sign because Sheila Potter, daughter of the owners, was in my class at Four Dwellings School. During the war we used to take 6d or 1s to school to buy savings stamps at 6d each, not so Sheila Potter; because her parents ran a business they must have been rich as Sheila came with a 10s note and had a whole certificate each week! I thought it would be a good idea to take a photograph before the name was covered for another fifty years.

Incidentally, the name 'Witcomb' appears very faintly under Potters. Could this have been their first premises?

Bryan Palser

Quinton love story

The following is the story of the early life of my grandfather, Philip Henry Birch (1880–1954). He farmed in Quinton at Ivy House, Castle and Perry Hill Farms.

My grandfather was eventually sent to work as a shop boy at Norton's Bakery in 392 Bearwood Road. I suppose he would have been about twelve to fourteen years old. A few years passed by, during which time he learnt the trade. He was sweet on the boss's daughter and what followed was something similar to a Victorian melodrama.

The stately Mr Charles Norton must have been shocked by the orphan shop boy's interest in his daughter. The story goes as follows: Mr Norton stated that if my grandfather wanted his daughter, then he must go out into the world and make his fortune. The figure quoted by various members of our family is £200 – truly a fortune in those days. Away he went. He joined the Army and I would suspect that they didn't expect to see him again.

He volunteered for the South African Light Horse Infantry, which saw a lot of action in the Boer War – The relief of Ladysmith and Mafeking, Tugela Heights, Orange River etc. He met Winston Churchill. After the war was over, he worked in the Kimberly Diamond Mines where I suspect he made his money. He returned to England in 1903.

Old Mr Norton kept his word; his daughter Winifred married Philip in 1904–05 after he helped out in buying Castle Farm in Warley. It was a success and after a year or two they moved to Perry Hill. They had three children; the first was my father, Philip Arthur Birch who was born on 31 January 1907.

By renting Ivy House farm to use as the dairy, the farm thrived. Eventually my father was given the milk round as a wedding present in 1929. The dairy side ceased and my

Potters, the butcher's sign, unveiled in 2004.

grandfather went into semi-retirement at Perry Hill. The ground was sold in 1937 for building, which is now Lewis Road and Barston Road as far as the bottom of what is now Kingsway. My grandparents lived out their lives at no. 10, the first house in Lewis Road. My grandmother died in 1952 and my grandfather later in 1954.

My father carried on milk deliveries until 1936, bottling milk collected daily from Tom Powell's farm at Shenley Court. Eventually he sold the business to The Midland Counties Dairy.

John Birch

Ye Olde Sweet Shop

The cottage in which the sweet shop was run is still there. As a child, in the 1930s, I used to visit it with my mother. The people who ran it, Mrs Taylor and her daughter, fascinated me; they both had goitres. I don't remember what was bought there but my sister writes that she remembers being taken there for vinegar – at that time there was a small low

The sweet shop in Hagley Road West, next door to the Kings Highway, *c.* 1952.

counter in the front room. The cottage was quite small and it had a Player's Navy Cut advertisement on the side.

The present owner bought the pair of cottages which were semi-detached thirteen years previously. His intentions were to knock them down and build an office block.

However, Birmingham and Halesowen gave permission, but Sandwell did not. I did not check but I think they probably are in Sandwell. The cottages were purchased from Mrs Taylor's son-in-law Major Edwards. He was in his nineties and died soon after. They are 199-years-old now and originally had thatched roofs.

Mrs Marjorie Berry (née Phillips)

Quinton Village Bobby

Until about the 1950s there was a small police station in one of those little houses on Hagley Road West between High Street and the school drive. The first policeman I remember was Joe Smith who was based there in the 1920s. Then there was PC Wiggin and later PC Bill Tarrant who had an allotment and was the village bobby till he retired.

Ron Smith

Pigs, chickens and horses

I remember some of the shops, such as Badger's ironmongers where Scriven's Estate Agents now stands; Jordan's cakeshop on the Midland Bank site and Hadley's baker's shop in Bissell Street where they made lovely crusty cottage loaves.

The Deeleys were still running the post office. There was a public telephone just inside. Also in Bissell Street was Mr Dugmore's factory where I had my first job at fourteen. I earned 10s a week. They specialised in enamelling work and chain-making.

Quinton's first library in Stoney Lane in the 1920s.

The chains were for hanging chandeliers. About twenty-five people were employed at the firm. There was a garden nursery – a sort of early garden centre where they sold some good quality plants. It had two or three large greenhouses. This too was in Bissell Street. Mr Guest was the village postman. He was the father of the Guest sisters who ran the laundry. He had a big white beard like Father Christmas.

When we moved to the 'outdoor', we kept pigs and chickens at the back. We had two horses stabled there as well. One belonged to Charlie Tustin who lived in Harborne but was a sweet factor in Halesowen. The other belonged to the daughter of Dr Mather, a local GP. He was a family friend and sometimes borrowed my father's gun for shooting trips. It was a double-barrelled shotgun, which my father treasured as it was a present from George Bellhouse, a well-known jockey at the time. I have no recollection of my father using it, though some other Quintonians were known to go out shooting in the surrounding countryside.

Winifred Courier

Quinton's first library

I have always loved reading and the library was in Stoney Lane on the same side as the Old Rectory just about where the scout hut is now. It was wooden; you entered via a few wooden steps and the books were on both sides and the lady used to sit at the end; the books were covered in a sort of leather material; they were mostly red or blue. I would always take out one or two books, usually romances.

I used to see this chap go in and wonder what he was reading; he was a few years older than me. So when I went in again I looked to see what books he was taking. Well they were Brett-Young and Charles Dickens, so I was introduced to those. Sometimes, he would

The nailer's cottage on the corner of High Street and Ridgacre Road, c. 1930. Frederick Round is standing at the gate.

walk me home. This was allowed because his father went to the Wesleyan Chapel and knew mother, so that was alright.

Mary Davis (*née* Watson)

Quinton's old nailer's cottage

I was born in 1930 in the cottage on the corner of Ridgacre Lane and High Street; there were eight of us: Mother, Father, two boys and four girls. Mrs Foley, who moved down to the Hollybush, left the nail house to my mom.

Inside the cottage was a dining room, the two out-houses or brewhouses where Mom would do her washing in the big copper where we used to light the fire underneath, every Monday morning. The other outhouse was on this side with the gas stove in there. Inside another room was the old grate with a frying pan hanging over it. The stairs were stone and eventually Mom had them covered with wood. The stairs have moved now, and aren't in the same place. There's a solid big room, with a little room next to it, a little passage along, then into the front room, which was in the High Street. The front room was very rarely used. The door that exists now was there but never used; there was another door on the right in Ridgacre Lane, now blocked off. People used to shelter under the yew when it rained – the one that has been chopped down.

There were beams upstairs; they say it is solid floors but I am sure it was timber. The walls are all false inside, it is all plastered, nothing like it was inside. The walls were about 2ft 6ins thick. The two lots each side were built on – where the porch is was just waste ground in High Street and there were two big rooms upstairs with a door in the middle. Mom had the one big room divided for the girls and boys; if you were cold you'd put another coat on the bed.

Times were hard then. When we were young, we hadn't got a light but we lived and we were alright. No electric in the cottage, only gas, everybody had gas, with the old mantles about 4d, and sometimes you would break it putting it up. We bought our mantles from the Fields sisters up High Street; the house is still there, from the bottom on the left-hand side where Shepherds was, and the space – they're building there. Fields' shop was on the right of the arch.

Mom was Lillian and Dad was Frederick. Dad died when I was six. He was thirty-nine; it was a struggle then and with no social security, Mom had to go to the parish. She didn't marry again. The rector then was Mr Palmer. It was a hard life though. Shepherds in the High Street bought the cottage in 1947 for £400 and we bought a house up Lightwoods Hill. Shepherd then sold it on to Arnold Parkes for £500 the day after so he made £100 profit in a day. Arnold put the windows out of the tollhouse in there.

Mom was happy with £400; she'd never seen that sort of money. Mom always wanted to get back to Quinton because she was born there.

John Round

Tales from the Graveyard

My dad was a postman later in life; he worked from the old sorting office to the rear of Nora Parkes' drapers shop. Before then he had several odd jobs, which he did to keep the family in food. One was as gravedigger at the old burial ground. We lived in High Street and my dad was bit of a gentleman; sometimes if he was feeling a bit scruffy he would climb over the wall to save him walking round and seeing someone. Sam Bissell, who lived at the top of the opening to the park in Meadow Road, was one of the trustees of the cemetery and he asked Dad to look after the ground and open up the graves for burials. As you go through the gates and down at the bottom of the path, Dad had a hut there where he kept his tools and things. It was a bit bigger than a watchman's hut; people would always be going round to ask Dad's advice about something or other. He had an old coke fire outside; sometimes he would take a frying pan to cook some bacon on. My dad was an old friend of Mr George Green, of Green's the solicitors. Mr Green lived in a large house opposite where the picture house is now by the Wesleyan chapel. At one time they used to compile a list of people who paid to have their graves looked after. My dad was told not to tend to the ones who weren't on the list as paid but he told Mother he would take no notice. He said, 'We didn't pay to come into the world so I don't see why we should pay to depart it.' The area was so tidy because they used to cut all the grass and look after the headstones and flowers. My job was to go round making sure that the flowers had water. The water tap and tub was at the bottom of the path, behind the wall, right behind where we used to live.

One thing I remember about the burial ground was that one of the Masters families used to do their courting there. They would sit on one of the gravestones at the bottom, the one that had a big angel on. Now my dad would have to make sure that everyone was out of the cemetery when he closed the gates on the evening, so sometimes he would have to call them to make sure they didn't get locked in. One morning when he went round to open up, Mrs Wood, who lived in the caretaker's house, stopped him. 'Mr Watson,' she said, 'you locked the young courting couple in last night and they had to climb over the wall and get Mr Wood to let them out.'

One day a man came round to our house on his bike; he needed to ask Dad if one of the graves was a two or three because someone had died and they had to be buried quickly. So Dad sorted it out and went round to the burial ground to dig the grave. Now it was late one night and Mom said, 'Mary, your dad's been a long time and he's not had his dinner; go and see where he is!' Most women would have shouted over the wall at the bottom of the garden, but not Mother; she was a bit quiet and reserved. Now I had never been afraid of the dark or the burial ground at night because I had always been with Dad. Anyway, I went down the path and get to the end of the wall and I shouted 'Dad!' 'Dad!' and again a little further along, 'Dad!' 'Dad!' Well suddenly up pops this head out of a grave and I jumped nearly out of my skin, but then he saw me. Well, I told Mom. Later we used to have this hymn in chapel: 'Up from the grave he rose', well it was all my mom and I could do not to laugh, thinking about my dad that night. When my dad stopped digging the graves, I think a Jimmy Went took over.

Mary Davis (*née* Watson)

So many shops

In 1950, we moved into a house in Kingsway. We were registered for our rations at Moyle's grocery shop on the corner of Walters Road and Hagley Road West, later Don Smiths.

I bought my meat at Hayes the butchers on the corner of Clydesdale Road where there were four enthusiastic and helpful young butchers, some just returned from the forces.

The Hollybush provided a wonderful range of shops: George Mason, Wrensons, Maypole and one other grocer, bread shops, butchers and greengrocers, two shoe shops, a wool shop, Boots the Chemist and Glarry's the ladies' dress shop. There were probably others that I can't remember but we certainly didn't need to go any further for our shopping. Of course, there was also Smith Brothers, that wonderful Aladdin's cave for wood, glass, paint, white-wood furniture and anything in the hardware line.

Nora Hyett

Mr and Mrs Jones standing in the garden at Gorsy Road with Tibbetts Farm in the background.

The no. 10 bus at Quinton Road West terminus outside the Co-operative stores, with a Bundy clock to the right of the bus.

Farm areas

Quinton had many farms; there was one at the back of the cinema in Quinton – my parents referred to it as Hagge Farm. I can remember going there to a horse show gymkhana sometime in the 1940s. The area was developed into a housing estate in the 1950s, with a new semi-detached house costing around £1,500.

Another farm was located where the Perry Hill Tavern public house now stands and this was known as Cooper's farm. A pond bordered the road where local children used to go fishing. Further down Perry Hill opposite Oak Road was Brennand's farm with fields as far as the pre-war houses in the Kingsway; the road wasn't cut through until the 1960s when Brandhall Estate was built.

Another not quite so well-known farm was Tibbetts. Our parents would take us for a walk in our best Sunday clothes through the farm. It was situated in World's End Lane and access was via a pathway by the side of the doctors and club in Faraday Avenue.

Mrs Sheila Joyner

Refuge at Parkes café

Arnold Parkes had a café in Hagley Road West at one time because when I first starting courting Jenny, I used to catch the night service bus back home. I would turn the corner at the bottom of Bissell Street, go right by the allotments, and where the Methodist church is now was the bus terminus; it had one of those Bundy clocks. One night I was a bit late and I missed the bus; well, they were every hour and the weather was bad so I thought I would go into Parkes café and have a cup of tea. It was still open, although well past midnight.

There was also a row of church cottages just round the corner, on the right in Ridgacre

College Road Methodist church, c. 1965.

Road, as it was then, but they were knocked down when they put the motorway through. Ridgacre Road was all one continuous road then, Stoney Lane to Ridgeway Avenue. It was all one road then they cut various bits off and it was called Ridgeway Avenue. Once an island was there with a telephone kiosk and a wooden seat where the old men from Quinton Hall sat during the day.

Harry Cook

A bit of a wide boy

Next door to the grocers in Hagley Road West was Rudges, the greengrocer; they also had the bike shop where you bought your oil. Where the gents hairdressers is now used to be a lady with a general store that sold custard ice cream. On the corner was Kings the butchers, next door was Uncle Arnold Price's, the greengrocers, he was what you might call

' a bit of a wide boy' during the war and made a lot of money; he was a bit of a lad with the ladies. On the opposite corner was a small place that sold shrubs and alpines.

The last shop on the left towards Bearwood was Dalloway's fish 'n' chips and on the opposite corner was Dalloway's the wet fish shop. He was there in all weathers with his beautiful marble slabs with all the ice cubes on, dressed in his blue and white-striped pinafore, his hands and face were as blue as blue could be with the cold.

On the other side of the road was Egglingtons, a fantastic toy and bike shop.

Brian Lee

Wiggins Recreation Ground

The old Quinton Park was a lovely walk on a Sunday evening; everyone used to have a walk on Sunday evening – up the Hagley Road and stop for a drink at the Bush. Another walk was to Quinton Park then down by Wiggins Recreation Ground towards Woodgate, past Bellis & Morecombe Sports Ground where Winchester Drive is and on to Watery Lane. Where Chichester Drive is now was a corporation nursery where they did all the trees. When it was closed in 1964-65, when the

expressway was built, anyone could go there and have a tree. Where the Scout hut is, there are those few houses facing Ridgacre Road then Chichester Drive goes down – well just there was a little driveway, one side of it was the Parks department and the other side was a lane down to Wiggins. Woodgate Valley was farmland; it was Nonsuch Farm. The other

The general store and tobacconist of Hannah Woodward on the corner of Hagley Road West and Kingsway, c. 1920.

Gwyneth Jones at the rear of 6 College Road in the 1950s.

Anna Woodward's huckster shop

My aunt had the shop where the Kings Highway is now, or just to the right of it, at the top of the Kingsway. She was Mom's sister; Anna Mullet was her maiden name. She married a Woodward and she had that shop for years, a hucksters shop they used to call it. She used to do the tea, 4d and 6d a can for the bus drivers and conductors. They used to turn round there; on College Road, just where the chapel is now, there used to be a Bundy clock there.

Tinkers Farm was further down because Joe Lowe had the old cottage right at the top of the Kingsway. There was a cottage, then a little narrow lane, then my aunt's shop was right on the main road where the little island is now at the top of Kingsway – it was right there. The shop was demolished in the late 1930s when the Kings Highway was built.

John Round

side of the Monarch was where Tom Knockers Wood was.

Irene Devereux and Bryan Palser

Woods family took over the nursery

My husband's parents used to live in the cottage next to the Red Lion. Their cottage was on a bank and their name was Wood. Then they moved to the nurseries up by the old Hollybush. The Woods family took over the nurseries until they widened the road to make it two-way. Mr Wood's father, who was ninety-five years of age when he died, owned 3 acres of land and four greenhouses 60ft long – his land reached to Harborne Lane.

Mrs Gertrude Wood

Charge for batteries

One of the Parkes families had the factories at the back of College Road. They used to charge the batteries for 4d – I think that's right. They had a daughter called Muriel; she used to run a wool shop with her husband but later they moved to Wales.

Mrs Joan Smith (née Clay)

four

Schooldays

A sweet reward

When I was a kid at school there was a sweet shop, just opposite the church, kept by a Mrs Rose whose husband Sammy Rose was a bricklayer. Mrs Rose had a pony and trap and she used to go into Birmingham to get her tobacco and sweets. She would probably take about an hour to get there. Today, a quarter of an hour and you're there aren't you?

In those days there were no cars and I used to have to go and catch the pony that was in a field down Stoney Lane, down Ridgacre. I used to go down there and catch the pony, bring him up, put the harness on and put him in the trap ready for her to drive off. 'Call on your way back from school!' she'd say.

Well of course I did and was given a big box of all sorts: toffees and chocolates, perhaps going a bit mouldy, but I was very popular with the kids at school.

Of course today everybody's got a car – even children have got cars. In those days nobody had a car; it was always horse and trap. The first mechanised vehicle I saw was a steamer that was used to deliver the flour. You had to have a licence in those days to drive a car or a bike and I think it was about five bob.

At the weekend I used to help Mrs Rose make ice cream; she'd give me a couple of ice pies. The machine I used had a container in the middle; it was a container inside a bigger wooden container that left about a 2-inch gap all around that you filled with ice. I had to keep sprinkling commercial salt on it and as it melted, it was intensely cold; the salt melted the ice and the handle got much harder to turn as the ice cream was nearly frozen. It was easy when I started but it became harder and

harder when it was nearly right – it was blooming hard work. When I'd finished, she gave me a spoon to eat the ice cream off the thing that rotated in the middle.

Cliff Smith & Smith Bros (Quinton) Archive

Handsworth Technical School

Four Dwellings School was really in the countryside because there was nothing built up around it; there was a lane down to Four Dwellings Farm and right opposite, on the corner, was Merris's farm. It was all fields as far as the junction of Gorsy Road and Quinton Road West. Opposite Four Dwellings School was a little raised area where we used to dig for pignuts.

I started school at Woodhouse Road and then moved to Four Dwellings on 1 July 1940; from there I went to Handsworth Technical School. At Four Dwellings we didn't have a uniform, just grey trousers and a grey shirt.

Bill Deeley

Four Dwellings Staff

The teachers at Four Dwellings School were Miss Lawdon, Miss Owen, Miss Fowler, Mr Ryman, Miss Peyton (who recently died), and Mr Murray. I was secretary at Four Dwellings when Mr Phipps was there; he was a rough sort of individual and he would come in to me and say: 'Come on woman! Let's do some work!'– you got used to it. Before Mr Phipps, Mr Murray was head and he was a perfect gentleman. Mr Musgrave, a deputy-head, was also the perfect gentleman. Mr

Licence No. _5648_

3251

Motor Car Act, 1903.

CITY OF BIRMINGHAM.

RENEWAL of LICENCE to DRIVE a MOTOR CAR or CYCLE.

James Dugmore

of _Bissell Street, Deriton Man_

is hereby Licensed to drive a MOTOR CAR or CYCLE for the period of Twelve

Months from the _3_ day of _December 19 20_

until the _2_ day of _December 19 21_ inclusive.

Date of issue _30/11/20_

J.H.C. Gillshie.

Acting Town Clerk.

N.B.—Particulars of any endorsement of any Licence previously held by the person licensed must be entered on the back of this Licence.

Fee, 5/-

A driving licence renewal for James Dugmore of Bissell Street in 1921.

A games lesson at Four Dwellings School in 1942.

Musgrave never got on with Mr Phipps; Phipps had come from Oozells Street, which was quite a rough school. If anyone had done something wrong he wouldn't cane them but make them stand outside his room for hours and hours or he would make them kneel down. Miss Grainger was really old, rotund with a round face and iron-grey hair. She had a bicycle, which she used to get one of the pupils to push up Ridgacre Road; she came from Woodhouse Road. Mr Ryman was head of infants during the day; he also had the largest classroom, then at night he played the piano in the Kings Highway; he used to come into school 'three sheets to the wind'.

Irene Devereux

Four Dwellings' opening

I began school at Woodhouse Road in 1939 and moved to Four Dwellings when it opened on 1 July 1940. I went to Monday evening school at what was World's End Lane Farm, which was turned into Quinton Evangelical church, and later to Sunday school at Quinton.

Mrs Palser walking in World's End Lane.

We used to walk down Watery Lane, pick blackberries and have a picnic – that was a day out for us. We used to play over the field, which was opposite the houses in Ridgacre Road. During the war it was used as a barrage balloon site. We used to play over there and the stream used to go through, I think at one time there were a few fishes. It was later culverted and Daventry Grove was built, the stream went under Ridgacre Road. The houses in Ridgacre Road didn't have garages because people didn't have cars.

We played in the right of way at the back and built little campfires. We came home from Four Dwellings via the right of ways, Higgins Lane and World's End Lane.

Before the war, coming home from Four Dwellings was across fields before the new estate was built in Warple Road, fifty years ago.

I played with a lad called Alan Burchell at Four Dwellings Farm, which was kept by Burchells.

Bryan Palser

Grammar school days

In those days it was quite something for 'Pop' to pay for us to go to the grammar school. We had quite a difficult written exam, followed by oral exams, but we had to pay because it was means-tested. My mother and father were Kathleen and Wilfred Ashman. In those days Mr Clark, Mr Ashman – my uncle – and Mr Cooper seemed to run everything in the village.

I used to have to walk from Victoria Avenue, which wasn't completely built up, to the Hagley Road to school. I remember that it was so hot; there were no buildings as such and no traffic. There was the old Stag pub right on the edge. When I went to grammar school I walked to Halesowen because I was given only 1s a week pocket money. So if I walked to Halesowen Grammar, I saved 1d

The Lapal School Coronation celebration photograph in 1937.

each way. My father objected to the school being called 'The Earls', so much so that he wouldn't give the 'old boys' speech any longer. Along Halesowen Road, on the left-hand side, roughly where Narrow Lane is, was Crock Street, a little row of old terraced houses. The convalescent home was there, and Greens the solicitors moved in there. He was the Black Country solicitor and he was doing quite well.

Dorothy Mason

Lapal Primary School

Sometime in 1948 I was off to school. I remember that Lapal Primary had a huge playing field and was near the Royal Oak at the bottom of Kent Road. You had to go through a narrow passageway to get to it though there was another entrance from Priory Road.

Time marched on and eventually the eleven plus exam loomed. Grammar school or sec-

ondary modern – which was it to be? My parents obviously wanted me to go to the grammar school and to that end I had additional lessons with a private tutor. I recall, rather hazily, that I went down Spies Lane to the Royal Oak and turned left and he lived in a house just down there on the right which must have been near Lapal Primary School. I cannot remember his name though. But it was all to no avail and so it was off to Hill and Cakemore Secondary Modern Boys' School in Long Lane.

Stuart Jones

May Day dancing

At school, once or twice a week, we would go into the parish hall for a class called music and movement. We did it to the sound of the BBC coming from a steam radio perched on the edge of the stage. We would prance about and have fun that children of today, aspiring disco divas that they are, would laugh at. We also did our May Day dancing here with no political overtones at all. In the middle of the hall there would be a square wooden post that would stand up on its own, having large feet at the bottom. It was probably used for netball at other times. At the top was a small pram wheel, tied to the rim of which would be about a dozen or more different coloured tapes. We would hold on to the ends of these tapes and dance round the pole in opposite directions, winding the tapes into pretty patterns. I can't remember the last time I saw such an activity.

There must have been some kind of craft class at school, for my other sister Vivienne still has a wooden box about 15in by 8in by 5in deep that I made there. Nothing so sophisticated as dovetail joints or glue, all butt joints and all nailed. The lid has a crayoned red cross on it outlined with the heads of small nails. So it must have been intended for use as a first aid box.

Phil Lamb

Miss Spackman

My first teacher at the church school was Miss Spackman who lived in Stennels Avenue (off Manor Lane). She was the teacher in the infants' class that I entered in 1935, at the age of five. My first classroom was in the building which is almost opposite the parish hall; it had a central door and rooms on either side. My classroom was on the left and had a fireplace with a big iron guard in the wall between the two rooms. I remember another infant teacher called Miss Ford, who later was married and became Mrs Ranford. She lived at the bottom of Walters Road on the left-hand side where it joins Kingsway. Both teachers were lovely and very well liked.

A few other teachers I recall from my school days were Miss Cutler; Miss Smart –red-haired and quick-tempered – who taught me to knit; Mr Ashman and the head teacher Mr Clarke.

I met Miss Smart in Netherton. I was in my thirties and working as a social worker in Dudley. She was retired and lived in Netherton. I recognised her instantly and spoke to her, and she remembered me. Not too long afterwards, I read of her death in the local paper as a result of a road accident.

Marjorie Berry (née Phillips)

Shaking the tray

On arrival at school every child was given a small metal tray into which was poured a small amount of silver sand. We were coached by the teacher to trace in the sand the letters of the alphabet, using the forefinger. Mistakes were easily rectified by shaking the tray. From this rudimentary beginning of 'the cat sat on the mat', the fundamental principles of the English language were learned.

Every child was in need of an afternoon period of rest. Children of another year, being stronger and more physically developed, were required to erect basic wooden makeshift beds upon which the younger children would repose in not-quite-silent bliss. After this rest period, the beds were returned to the place from whence they came and the education process continued.

Denis Colclough

Mr Burns

I was educated at the church school at the rear of the church. I left school in 1912. Mr Burns was the headmaster, a much-bearded gentleman who lived in the last house below The Green, just beyond the entrance to the park.

At the church school I was, for a time, a friend of Edwin Danks. His father lived on the opposite side of Hagley Road to his grandfather whose house occupied the site of the Essoldo.

We used to borrow his father's golf clubs and go over to Brandhall golf course. No, not as you may conjecture, to play golf but to try and pinch player's 'lost' balls and then sell them to their owners in order to get some Woodbine money for ourselves.

I remember two of my heart-throbs in class: Maisie Tranter whose father kept Hole Farm and Edith Harborn whose father owned the nurseries in Bissell Street.

Harvey Johnson

Miss Spackman, *c.* 1936.

Dinner categories

Just outside was a house in which lived the church verger, Mr Ball. To get to the new building, you had to walk around to the back of the old one, passing alongside the church-yard wall, and then turning right. You would continue past some allotments and gardens on the left with the parish hall beyond, and the new building would be facing you. This building was also used for school dinners.

We would queue up, standing against the wall waiting for Mrs Parry to collect our dinner tickets, green ones marked with a large bold capital P or F. If yours had on it an F then you kept it hidden, not wanting others to know that your dinner was free as your parents could not afford to pay.

Phil Lamb

Evacuated school

Woodhouse School opened in 1931. I was five in July 1934. I assume that I started after the summer holidays in 1934. The headmaster was Mr Rand, the teachers I remember were Miss Heath, Miss Richards, Miss Swain and Mrs Cookson, and Mr Len Ryman came a little later. I believe Mr Ryman later moved to

Four Dwellings as deputy head. The chapel in Harborne, on the corner of Earls Court and Court Oak Road, was used as an overspill; it was run by two teachers, Mr Powell and Mr Beaumont.

I then went to Five Ways Grammar School in 1940; the school was evacuated to Monmouth. I really enjoyed my time down there and came back in 1943. I go to the reunion every year and went back in 2003 to celebrate its sixtieth birthday. My father was asked to do Father Christmas in the mid-1950s and Miss Heath was still on the staff.

My one memory was the first day at school; I came home at lunchtime and hid in the coal-house. I went back to Woodhouse fifteen years ago; it hadn't changed much. They had built a couple of classrooms over to the left; it used to be a wooden building that they used for school dinners. When I was at Woodhouse, Overdale Road was just being built and there was no entrance to the school in Ridgacre Road, the only entrance being Woodhouse Road.

John Birch

Mrs Parry and the class of 1964 at Quinton Church School.

My gingham school dress

During the Easter school holidays it was time for a trip to the big city to purchase the material for my summer dress. I had only one dress for the whole summer term because it could always be washed and dried overnight. Mom would say: 'I've never seen anyone wearing two frocks!'

We went straight to the Bullring market to purchase 2 yards of coloured gingham at 6d a yard. If you were lucky you could get it for 4d with cotton, and for a few coppers more, with binding.

Next was Woolworths to get ½lb of cream biscuits for special occasions at 4d, and also ½lb of broken biscuits at 2d a pound. The next shop to visit was Peacocks for some interlock underwear that cost about 2s or 3s.

Next day, the material was taken in Mom's basket, always covered with a white tea towel – whatever was in the basket – to Auntie Etty who would make the material into my new summer dress. We would be able to collect the new dress a week later: 'No charge!' said

Mom, 'Money doesn't grow on trees – there's a depression'.

Mom would go home to cook the tea but she would leave me with 6d to go to Mr and Mrs Thatcher's cottage close to The Slyng. I had to go and get my posh haircut; the big chop took place in the doorway of their cottage. Mr Thatcher was the barber at Quinton Hall, the old men's home.

Gladys Jones

Church of England school

I remember dancing around the maypole to an *English Country Garden* and Handel's *Water Music*, accompanied by Mrs Williams. We would either perform in the church hall or on the grass at Quinton Hall. I loved plaiting the ribbons up the pole into tight knots but hated prancing around holding a girl's hand.

The annual Christmas plays were held in the school hall. These were packed to the rafters with an audience of parents eager to see their darlings perform. The children could not see anyone because of the overpowering lights.

I played Old King Cole in Class One, and danced around his Christmas tree (Joseph Hathaway). Christopher Banner, Matthew Whitehouse, Kevin Durrell and myself gave a rather splendid Cossack dance. Mark Ashworth was an exceptional harlequin but the leotard was so comical.

Christmas parties were in the school hall. Nelson Nelson − was that really his name? − from the church dressed as Father Christmas. Mr Brett also had a go at Santa but was too easy to recognise.

There were Nativity and Easter performances in the church; I was one of the shepherd extras without a speaking part. Harvest festival was also in the much-used church. My marrow, inscribed every year with 'God is Love', was nestled in a heap of tinned fruit and tins of spam.

Autumn meant prizes were given for the 'autumn collections'. Bark, dead leaves in various hues, nuts and acorns were gathered by family expeditions to the rural areas such as Warley Woods, Lickey Hills, Clent Hills and Frankley Beeches. These were then attached to card with copious blobs of fish-paste glue and long brushes. The chances of winning the certificate were enhanced by the variety of material presented and not by re-using last year's mouldy effort.

St George's Day was the day the Cub Scouts and the Boys' Life Brigade were allowed to wear their uniforms. This lead to huge rivalries between opposing troops. The Girl Guides and the Girls' Life Brigade joined in too. Unfortunately, we were not allowed to display our marching skills across the crowded playground. God Save the Queen with the extra verses was the usual hymn in assembly. My Boys' Life Brigade uniform originally had round sailor hats that were the British answer to the Frisbee. We had a white rope − whitened with talcum powder and smelling sweetly − noose around our necks and sown into our chest badges. No wonder the uniform was later replaced by a safer style with a rather fetching blue Thunderbirds cap.

Quinton Hall hosted the sports day under the curious gaze of the elderly residents. There was a six-lane running track laid out for an imperial 100ft up the lawn. This provided the course for the flat, three-legged, wheelbarrow, sack and the hard-boiled egg and spoon races. Only a few dared enter the endurance race that went twice around the oval track. Jeremy Parker, who was my junior, beat me in my last year denying me a clean sweep. Our mothers then embarrassed us by staging their own race. I amassed a sizeable collection of first-, second- and third-place badges.

Geoff Broughton

Quinton Preparatory School

Quinton Preparatory School was situated at Forest Road and Oak Road, which were at that time in the district of Quinton. It was a small, fee-paying, junior school with an excellent reputation and was run by three very Victorian maiden ladies named Wharf. Miss Vera, the oldest, was the headmistress and was therefore known as Miss Wharf. Her two younger sisters were Miss Fanny and Miss Phyllis. Miss Phyllis was the youngest and cuddliest; she was the one who could be relied upon for comfort and sweets in times of trauma. She also taught the nice things which were connected with plasticine and paint. The other two sisters, ably assisted by a very formidable lady called Mrs McKay, taught the more serious subjects. Mrs McKay was the maths teacher and lived somewhere in the vicinity of White Road.

Mrs Maudsley and the Revd Compton opening a church fete. Seated are Mr and Mrs Keyte and Mr and Mrs Penny.

Christ Church Scouts, *c.* 1950.

The uniform was navy and black with red blazers and a school badge of intertwined QPS in gold. The ties were red with gold and black stripes. The girls wore pink and white gingham dresses in the summer and the boys wore grey trousers.

QLHS Archive

Red exercise books

We all went to Quinton Church School; Mr Ashman was a lovely man, the deputy head under Mr Clark, the headmaster. Miss Smart had red hair; she was a terror and she would hit you round the head or bang your heads together.

We had inkwells and we would write with pen and ink; there was a groove in the desk where you would put your pen and a hole for the inkwell. In the room where Mr Ashman taught was a desk that had a little slot in it;

that was when the children used to have to pay to go to school and they used to put the money in the slot.

We had red exercise books with our times tables on the back and we had to learn our tables off by heart.

In the early 1920s, they introduced a third of a pint of milk for 1d. The cardboard disk that was on the top of the bottle would be taken off and dried and then you would wind wool around and cut it and make pompoms. If you took sandwiches for your dinner you would have to sit in the little cloakroom and eat them.

Mrs Wood was the school caretaker who lived in the house next to the school; she would let us have hot water to put on our Oxo cube.

You went to school at nine o'clock and you would have a quarter of an hour for your break; you came out at twelve o'clock for your

Quinton Church School, c. 1924.

Quinton Church School in the 1950s.

dinner and went back at 1.30 p.m. You would be in class for half an hour, have another little break then you would finish at 3.30 p.m., although seniors left at four o'clock.

Lessons would be sums, English, the girls would do cooking and the boys gardening, and we would have games. The toilets are still there that were used in the 1920s.

Joan Clay, Lucy Dearn, Gladys Jones and Lawrence Basterfield

First day at school

The school was a brick-built Victorian building with some Gothic windows. The infants' classroom was a separate building but was close to the junior school. The playgrounds were blue brick and the toilets were out of doors, across the playground next to the cemetery wall. All was situated behind the church, well back from the busy main road. Big iron gates, dark blue in colour, closed off the playground and path. A policeman, Mr Banyard, manned the Belisher crossing outside the school gates every day and saw us safely across the road.

Miss Ford took me to the infants' class. She had a pretty freckled face, dark curly hair and a cheery, jolly, energetic manner. She always wore gym shoes, a dark skirt and a bright, flowery, overall top. She played the piano well. It was a large class of about forty children. She seated me in a double desk next to a little blond boy called Philip Riley. She then called the register and we were told to answer 'Yes Miss Ford,' when she called our names. We were given a tin of plasticine, a small hand-held blackboard, some chalk and a blackboard rubber. I do not remember using paper, pencils, crayons or paint whilst I was in that class. Written work, maths and most of the art work were all done on our blackboards. We were given coloured chalks to colour in our pictures and plain white was used for the more formal lessons. Some maths and artwork was done using squares of sticky-backed, brightly coloured paper, which we cut into shapes with little rounded scissors.

Charlotte Tate (*née* Masters)

five

Work, Rest and Play

A 1900s night out

A night out included a seat at the theatre, also a meal, drinks plus sweets and ice cream for less than 10s. More fun was enjoyed if you went with a couple of friends to the Hippodrome, the Empire, the Grand Theatre or the Gaiety in Dale End or the Metropole Theatre at Snow Hill. You had a seat in the gallery or the gods for 3d and then after a fish 'n' chip supper for 3d.

There were penny concerts at Digbeth Institute in Deritend at the bottom of the Bull Ring, and also at the Old Temperance Hall in Temple Street. The artists were Will Gardiner, Percy Edwards and Percy Egar.

At Curzon Hall, for silent film at the Kings Hall in Corporation Street, the price was 2d for matinées and 4d in the evening; you could watch the pictures over and over again for that money, and showing were Cowboys and Indians, drama, comics and the ink well drawings. Theatres in Birmingham in the 1900s were Prince of Wales in Broad Street; Theatre Royal in New Street; The Alexandra in John Bright Street; the Tivoli Empire in Hurst Street; Bordesley Palace in Digbeth, off Coventry Road; the Metropole or the Blood Tub at Snow Hill, and Aston Hippodrome, the Aston Theatre Royal and the Gaiety Theatre in Coleshill Street. There were also over twenty picture houses. The first talkie was at the Futurist in John Bright Street with Al Jolson singing *Sonny Boy*.

The old silent films were on the way out; the next talk was at the old West End picture house, which was the old Curzon Hall. In the 1900s there were circuses held at Catlins Perriotts. Lilly Manders was a female imper-sonator and also a very good dancer. Many artists started there such as Will Gardiner, Sid Field who lived in Sparkbrook and also Percy Edwards the birdman.

Mrs Helen Cooper

An important means of communication

I spent twenty-seven years of my life in Wilmington Road. On the corner of Wilmington Road and Hagley Road West was a telephone kiosk, which was a very important centre of communication; in those days a telephone in one's home was a luxury. From this kiosk, we, as children and later as teenagers, would be able to access the world. In those days, this stretched to Harborne, Halesowen or the city centre and, of course, those other environs where one had a friend or relation.

Social outings to places like coffee bars or the ice rink, cinemas and youth clubs, and dates with members of the opposite sex would not have happened without this telephone kiosk. Even when the home telephone became more readily available, the use of the kiosk did not decline. It was still used to plan one's social life without the presence of parental interference.

Before the charging structure of telephones became complex one could, provided it was a local call, talk as long as one wished for 2d.

At one time, I held the school record for one continuous call: an hour and forty-three minutes. It would have been longer but someone else was waiting to use the phone – not for the whole time, I hasten to add.

Keith McDonald

Mrs Ruffles and party at the old Quinborne Centre in Ridgacre Road in the mid-1940s.

Heart-throbs

Entertainment apart from the cinema seemed to be mainly horse shows and gymkhanas – sometimes in Lightwoods Park or in the fields near Hagge Farm.

The head boy at school was a hero of mine and at a hobbies competition at school he won a prize for his collection of rosettes won at horse shows.

A circus also came to Hagge Farm – Little Sylvia's. She may have owned it but she certainly did most of the work – helping to put up the tent, perform on the trapeze and ride bareback on the horses. She was little but must have been very strong. A special treat was The Norton Follies, an Army entertainment show, which came from Norton Barracks near Worcester and, once more, performed in a large tent at Hagge Farm. All the entertainers were men and presumably soldiers. One of them was Frederick Ferrari who later appeared with Charlie Chester. I particularly liked their rendition of the Quartet from *Rigoletto* – all male and very amusing. More heart-throbs! Entertainment at home, apart from piano playing and reading, came from the radio with programmes such as *I.T.M.A.*, *Henry Hall's Guest Night* and *Saturday Night Theatre*. I was usually asleep curled up in a chair before the end. There were also classical music concerts at Birmingham Town Hall.

Mrs Marjorie Berry (*née* Phillips)

Quinton Colts football team after a friendly with Bournville in October 1950.

Fred Hobson's band

I was very interested to find the photograph of Fred Hobson's band in the *Quinton* book. My family knew Fred and his wife when they lived at 19 Glyn Road. Fred played in a hall along the Bearwood Road in Smethwick. Once a year he held a dance competition at the Smethwick baths. During the winter the baths were covered over and a lovely dance floor was laid or suspended. It was a very glittering occasion and attracted dancers such as Peggy Spencer from London; it was just like *Come Dancing* on the television. I believe Fred Hobson didn't know a note of music but was responsible for organising a dance band, as he thought it was needed in the area.

Joyce Barber

The golf house reception

When I was at Woodhouse, Overdale Road was just being built; there was no entrance to the school in Ridgacre Road, the only entrance being Woodhouse Road.

The old golf house was still there a long time after Overdale Road was finished. In fact my sister, who got married in 1952, used the golf house for the reception. The golf course went as far as World's End Lane and bordered on to White Road.

I remember the coronation party in 1937 and coming home with my mug.

John Birch

Quinton Colts

Between 1950 and 1953, I played football for Quinton Colts with our home games being played at Quinton Park where we were always well supported by the residents of the nearby old men's home. We held our own as far as results were concerned, with the team selection being made during the week in the milk bar opposite the Danilo.

Gilbert Spurr, who lived in Victoria Road in Quinton, initiated Quinton Colts and, for 1s per week, we were supplied with our kit, ground hire, and referee's expenses – I cannot recall having to pay for any coach hire. If we did have to pay, it wouldn't have been very much.

After all I only had 10s for the week when I was working and 2s 6d when still at school. As for Quinton Park, it had one football pitch, two tennis courts, changing rooms that were never vandalised, and a footpath running from end to end. The tennis courts were very popular and had to be booked in advance during holidays and weekends to guarantee a game.

The main problem was finding new players because of the demands of national service. Some team members I remember are: Gilbert Spurr, George Williamson, Terry Jones, Peter Reynolds and Roger Hughes.

Another team that played in Quinton Park was the Quinton Rangers.

Brian Jones

Fosters in Bearwood

I used to work part-time at Fosters in Bearwood on the corner of Anderson Road, because they hadn't got any men. They'd never employed women; in fact the only woman employed by Fosters was the cashier. I only wish I had a picture of the inside of that shop with the cash track – I would place the money in the container, screw the little cup up, pull the handle, and it shot along the track towards the girl in her office. She would take the money and send the container with the

change and the bill back to the assistant to give to the customer.

Mrs Eileen Lee (née Clark)

£5 per week pay

When I left the Army I drifted around in various jobs for a few years until I joined the fire service in 1952. I did twenty-seven years service and retired in 1979.

When Joyce and I got married in 1953 the pay was £4 17s 6d. Joyce was working at the telephone house and her wages were £3 10s 0d.

We went on our honeymoon to London in December 1953 and came back with 4d to start married life. We were allocated a bedsit in the station, at 15s 2d per week. In 1957 we were allocated a flat where we stayed for seventeen years, until we moved to Quinton.

John Birch

Phillit Quick Pump

The first job we had was from a friend of my dad's, a chap named Jim Parkes; he made pumps – what they called a Phillit Quick Pump. That was a pump with a tube inside a tube, you pulled the inside tube up and as you pushed it back down, it put so much in the tyre and so much in this other tube above. As you pulled it up you put the rest in, under pressure, so you didn't waste your energy. He had a bigger version, what they called a Garage Pump, which was made in brass and packed in cases – nice varnished cases. He asked me to put a price in for it, which I did; I ended up doing hundreds of these bloomin' pump boxes.

There was a wooden handle which had to be unscrewed to go into the box, but that still left a part sticking out, the part that the handle screwed into, so we had to cut a part out of

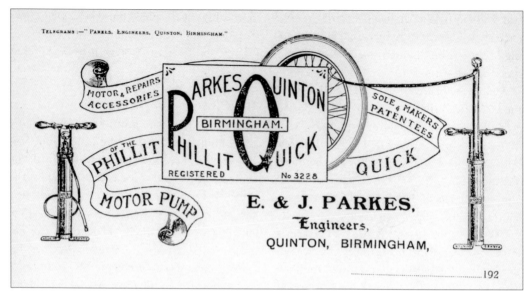

E. & J. Parkes' letterhead showing the famous Phillit Quick Pump logo.

the box. Well we got a gas engine to cut the wood up, and got a saw bench with a sort of fretsaw with a belt on it. It was only a fretsaw with a little blade but it didn't half travel at a speed, slick and smooth. We used to break saws by the dozen, but Stan and Ran worked on it – in fact Mother used to help us some-times because we had long pieces of timber delivered. To work these long pieces, we cut a slot in the side of the garage and Mother used to come along when we were cross cut-ting; we did everything on this saw, it was a rip saw but we made it cross cut, do anything, and Mother used to feed the timber in because you couldn't do it on your own. If Stan and Ran were out Mother used to come and help me to cut the stuff off.

Cliff Smith and Smith Bros Family Archive

Quinton Park

I was born in 1931 at 509 Ridgacre Road in Quinton. Quinton Park stretched from Good-rest Avenue up to Quinton. A fence ran on the extreme left-hand side as you looked towards the houses in Meadow Road. On the left-hand side by the third tree up, tennis courts were erected and just above them on the right-hand side and in the bushes were the toilets, the ladies' on the right and the men's on the left, and a path led from those toilets to an entrance in Meadow Road.

To the right-hand side of the park was a football pitch. On the left-hand side was a low fence which separated the park from Quinton Hall grounds. If you stand at the top by the manse you can see where the park was and the bottom part in Goodrest Avenue is still there. The left-hand side where the tennis courts were was made into a play area and a concrete base stands where the tennis courts were orig-inally. Beyond the first tree and the bushes was a shelter – the swings were in front.

Behind Hazel Stirrup's bungalow and Clay's house was what must have been a small quarry; it was called the valley. You came out from the valley and through the double gates that led into the road at the bottom. There was nothing on the left-hand side of the road except the fire station, which was a low building. Further on the left, in Quinton Hall grounds, were pigsties.

At the very bottom of Meadow Road, on the right-hand side, was a gate; this was situated where the T-junction is now with Chichester Drive. This gate led into the field where the football pitches were. There was also an entrance through to a little path where you could walk from Ridgacre Road to the allotments and Wiggins Recreation Ground.

On the right, at the bottom of Meadow Road, the land gradually went down into a dip; this led to a big pool where we used to go for tadpoles. The houses on the right of Meadow Road are new, the part where Hazel Stirrup used to live; there was a cow shed there.

Anthony Armstrong

I longed to ride

Joe and Hilda Lowe ran a dairy at the old farmhouse that was on the corner of Hagley Road West and the Kingsway. A riding school was started from the old barn attached to the farmhouse, the entrance being at the back, off Kingsway, where there is a small car park now. There were about five horses there and I longed to be allowed to learn to ride as I saw them going out across the Brandhall fields, or up Walters Road and down Stoney Lane to the lanes in the Four Dwellings area. My chance came when I left school in July 1945 and started to earn some money. Quinton was still very much a rural area at this time with fields and lanes to ride over. There were owls in the churchyard trees which we heard hooting and we saw a weasel in our side entry, presumably attracted by the aroma of my pet white mice.

For a time I had a soldier penfriend called Gilbert Geddes. I've no memory of how pen-friendships happened but they were very popular.

Mrs Marjorie Berry (*née* Phillips)

Stan Smith the athlete

My brother Stan won the Polytechnic marathon; in those days the Polytechnic was the unofficial world championship and all the best in the world used to compete: the Japanese, South Africans, Americans – and Stan beat them all. Stan used to run a lot of 10-mile races for Birchfield Harriers; he ran in the National but he thought he'd try his hand at marathon running.

He went up to Sheffield and he got a third, and he went on to Boldere and did even better with a second so he thought he'd enter the Poly, which would have been out of his class normally.

There was a hell of a field in the race which was run from Windsor Castle to Stamford Bridge. Stan managed to get up to a little knot of winners all running together, past winners and record holders, about six of them running together. He ran with them until about the 20-mile post and he thought, 'Well, they ain't going fast enough,' so he went, he passed them and they were saying: 'Smith? Never heard of him.'

He only went and won it – he actually won it. It was a sensation at the time; that's when he got picked for England and he ran for England in Canada at the Empire and Commonwealth Games.

We used to have an annual relay race, from Halesowen to Bewdley – well it started off at Stourport then they changed it to Bewdley. In this particular year, I ran the last leg for the winning team. There were four of us, doing about 4 miles apiece, but Stan starts for them and he goes all the way on his own. Don't forget we've got four blokes running ours and I ran the last

Above Air Training Corps of the 486 Quinton Squadron at RAF Peplow in August 1944.
Opposite Stan Smith winning the London Polytechnic Marathon.

leg for the winning team and continued running across the bridge, which was just after the finishing line. I ran across the bridge because our coach was stopped the other side of the bridge with all our clobber aboard. I turned round and Stan was coming in second; if the race had been much longer he'd have caught me and he ran all the way – amazing.

Ran was a good miler; I won a few mile races, but I wasn't in the same street as Stan. He was very difficult to beat; if you'd go fast he'd go fast, if you went slow he'd go slow, he was always tip-tap, tip-tap, tip-tap, right behind you on your shoulder. If you went fast or you went slow he was still there, it didn't make any difference.

Cliff Smith and Smith Bros Family Archive

Time, gentlemen, please!

In 1928, my family and I moved into a newly built house exactly opposite the Red Lion. It then stood on what is now the 18ft bank on the carriageway going towards Birmingham.

The pub stood so near to the house, No. 624, that we could hear the landlord calling 'Time, gentlemen, please!' from the kitchen.

All around was fields as far as you could see. You could walk across to Woodgate without touching a road.

Miss E. Kesterton

Trooping the Colour

During the latter part of the war, I enrolled in the Air Training Corps in 1943 with the 486 Quinton squadron. At that time there were about 100 cadets in the squadron. We used to meet at Four Dwellings School on Tuesday and Thursday evenings for class work and on Sunday mornings for parades. We had quite a good drum and pipe band, which was used for church parades round the village to Christ Church.

We had a very good warrant officer who had served in the Sherwood Foresters. He taught us our rifle drill and 'square bashing', which was put to good use when the squadron was the very first in the country to be presented with colours. We then had a Trooping the Colour ceremony, which was performed at Quinton Hall, now long since demolished. The colours were kept at Quinton Church. The rector, Mr Palmer, was our padre. They have since been moved to RAF Cosford for safekeeping.

Whilst with the ATC, we used to go to RAF stations for flying trips, usually on Sundays, and as often as not to Elmdon Airport in Birmingham. This was where the pilots had their initial flying training on Tiger Moths.

Each year there was an annual camp, normally at a bomber station, where we would fly in Wellingtons or Lancasters. These camps were a good time for learning how the air-crews and ground staff were trained and a good insight into armament, parachutes, rigging, aircraft electrics, and radios, etc. When the war finished in 1945, the interest waned a little and attendances fell.

At this point 486 Quinton merged with 485 Harborne and 2016 Weoley Castle Squadrons to form 485 Harborne and Quinton Squadron; for a time we had a very large band with three bass drums and Church parades were quite a noisy affair.

Clive Davies

Fire service equipment

When the blitz was on Coventry, the men from the station went there on occasions and other stations came here. During the war, all of the fixtures and fittings were different. The hydrants and the fittings were different in Birmingham to those in Coventry, Oldbury or Wolverhampton. Our fittings were 3½in whereas other brigades could have been 3¾ or

4in. When the National Fire Service began in 1940, the first thing they did was standardise all the equipment. When the war started, the service was known as the AFS, the Auxiliary Fire Service, but later it became nationalised and became the NFS, the National Fire Service, until it was handed over to the Civic Authorities in 1946-47.

The Rose Road fire station was the regular fire station, but the NFS took over various big houses and turned them into fire stations during the war; there were several in Harborne: Wentworth Road and Somerset Road being two examples. There must have been one or two in Quinton but I can't recall where; all over the place, as well, they had big static water tanks.

The 'open boat' fire engines of the 1930s were old Leylands. During the war they used all sorts of things; a lot of the fire engines then were trailer-pumps and would use lorries and vans to pull the things. They were called Coventry Climax, a wonderful light and adaptable pump – in fact two men could move it round on two wheels. You could pump it for days and days; all you needed was the petrol and it would go on forever. There were no escape ladders on the open boats like there were afterwards. All we had on that was a 30ft extended wooden ladder which was strapped to the sides. They were very heavy and made of Columbian Pine; it took three or four men to get them up. Later, there was a 60ft escape ladder on the Bedford which you see on the right of the picture. The Bedfords only did about 4 or 5 miles to the gallon, but all of the equipment ran on the petrol.

John Birch

To be a mechanic

When I left school, I wanted to be a mechanic but the war was on. My mother tried every-

Birmingham AFS Red Watch, c. 1954.

where to get me a job; I went to Mr Harrington, down by the Hollybush. He said he would train me but the war was on and by the time I was ready I would be going into the forces and it wouldn't be worth his while, so I looked around and went to Perry's Dairy in Meadow Road to drive a horse and cart to deliver the milk.

It was all right at the dairy but when I was seventeen, they did away with the horses and I had to learn to drive. Then I went to work for Halesowen Council and stayed there till I retired.

Lawrence Basterfield

A bad time to start

I'd always intended to go off on my own from when I was a kid, as soon as I could. In fact I started doing jobs at fourteen and the first job I did was a boiler lid for the mother of a pal of mine. I was at Phipps at the time and managed to get a few ⅝in boards, with a nice handle, and I think I charged her about 7s 6d. She was very pleased with it.

Smith Bros started in the early 1930s, working from home in Dad's garage; it was rather a big garage. It was in the Depression, a bad time to start. We paid ourselves thirty bob each a week, we kept ten bob and give a

Girls working in the offices of Smith Bros of Quinton on Hagley Road West.

pound to Mother, she had three quid. Then when we started to do better we paid ourselves fifty bob; we had a pound and Mother had thirty bob.

While I was still working at Phipps, I put our first workshop up, in the garden; Dad had some tons of ashes tipped because the ground sloped. I levelled it off then mucked the floor down; it was 30ft x 13ft, which was a good size at the time. I put the floor down first, then made the sections on the floor; Mum and Dad helped me to erect it but I made them on my own.

Then later on we had our first proper workshop and managed to arrange enough money to get the steel frame up, then filled the rest in. That was 60ft x 30ft, our first workshop.

Cliff Smith

Wellingtons for beer

When I left school, Dad got me a job at the income tax offices at 61 High Street in Old Hill. I worked with Mr Owen; he was never there, he used to visit the barber's daily. At the end of the day, I used to have the money; I'd put it in the books and take it down to Lloyds to bank. I was only sixteen and for that I had £1 per week.

I had to record all the money and one day the inspector came along. He said, 'You've got your accounts wrong.' We had five different books, schedule A, B, C, D and E, different taxes entered in all the books. Burton and Delinpoles had a 'doubt' going back to 1900 – they had been defrauding the country of tax; there were five of them and two committed suicide because of the money they owed.

I wanted to be a doctor but I got my diploma and became a teacher. My first school was in Lawrence Lane in Old Hill opposite the church.

One day I remember a boy didn't come into school so I recorded him absent in the register; he had no shoes to wear so I got him some wellingtons. The following week he was absent again so I asked him why; his mother had sold his wellingtons for beer. My wages at school were about £39 when I retired.

Horace Wilson

Five shillings a week

My sister and I went to Castle Road School first; we used to walk up Gateley Road or Frederick Road and across the fields up to the water tower, before the Wolverhampton Road was cut in 1927. When we were nine we left that school and moved to Quinton Church School; my sister was two and a half years older than me.

When I left school I went to a house in High Street in Harborne, just about where Boots is now. There was a doctor's house, then a big house where a Molly Griffiths had a flat. I learnt dressmaking with about four others. We earned about 5s per week for the first year then 12s 6d for the next year and 25s in the final year.

After my apprenticeship had finished I wasn't really wanted so I didn't get another job; instead I left work and did dressmaking from home.

Lucy Dearn

Milk and eggs

In the summer, keeping milk fresh was a problem; a lot of people bought the sour milk to make their own yoghurt. We fetched about fifty gallons every evening at about seven o'clock seven days a week from Shenley Farm. We bottled it up till about eleven o'clock at night; I was only six or seven. In the morning before I went to school I used to wash about 300 milk bottles.

We had a big galvanised bosh, put the empties in, and washed the bottles by hand. Then we had a bench with rows and rows of wooden pegs, which we put the bottles upside down to drain on, then bottled the milk by hand with measures; we would then press the cardboard tops on, not too hard or we would push them into the bottle. The cardboard top had a perforated middle, which we would press down and push our finger in and press the centre out.

Ernie Harwood with his dog at the rear of 28 Frederick Road.

Above A horse and cart delivering milk from the premises of Perry's Dairy in Meadow Road.

Left Wacaden's Dairy cap badge.

A quart of milk was 2d or a pint was 1¼d; a large loaf was 3½d, not sliced. We got our bread from Powell's in Harborne and the eggs from Stephenson's farm in Shenley Lane. We had a few eggs off a chap called Freddie Jones who kept pigs and fowl in Tennal Road.

On a Saturday morning we would go to a milk bottle rescue centre. We would take all our 'foreigners' here and change them for our own. We had about 500 bottles; they were embossed with P.A. Birch Harborne, with 'milk, butter and eggs' in the circle.

I spent the first two or three years of my life at school with bandages on my hands because of the cuts from the broken bottles. As we sold eggs, our old man wouldn't let us have a proper egg for breakfast; we had to have the cracked ones. People would knock on the door for cracked eggs because they were cheaper.

Merris' was on the corner of what is now Ridgacre Lane and Quinton Road West. It was one of the many dairies in Quinton at the time. There was ours, Bache's, Merris', Perry's, Wacaden's and of course the Co-op. Most of the deliveries when I was a lad were made by a horse and cart.

John Birch

The lorry collection

My dad, Arthur William Hill, worked for Wacaden Dairy. The Wacaden name stood for Wathes, Cattel and Gurden and they had a dairy in Frederick and Gateley Road in Quinton.

The offices were in Frederick Road, on the top right where the houses are set back. You turned right then first right into Gateley Road then there were yards and stables. The horses, carts and milk-bottling plant was kept there although originally the milk was delivered in a horse and cart and ladled into the customer's jug.

When Dad worked for them he collected the churns of milk from the farmers at Evesham on his lorry and took them to the Nova Scotia Street depot in Birmingham.

My dad was an employee for many years and his father before him. Mr Gurden was his godfather. I have a cap badge; his uniform was a blue all-in-one but I believe the milkman's uniform and the horse and cart livery was cream and green.

During the war, at Easter time you couldn't get chocolate eggs so the ladies at the farms used to paint rabbits on eggs for the children.

Mrs Jean Sunderland (*née* Hill)

Mr Stait, dressed in a white overall, in his shoe repair shop, 584 Hagley Road West, in 1956. Next door is Harrington's motor garage; Ken Field is the man on the motorbike.

Miss Eva Noble

PRINCIPAL OF THE

PARAMOUNT
SCHOOL OF DANCING

(HUDDERSFIELD)

WILL OPEN A DANCING SCHOOL
IN THIS DISTRICT AT

High Tors Commercial College

Perry Hill Road, QUINTON

Commencing, Monday 16th January

CLASSES WEEKLY AS FOLLOWS—

CHILDREN:

10 to 14 . Monday at 7-0 p.m.

3 to 10 . Saturday at 10-30 a.m.

ADULTS : Monday at 8-0 p.m.

Young Mens Tap Class . . . .

. . . . . . Monday at 9-0 p.m.

ALL CLASS LESSONS 1/6
PRIVATE LESSONS . by Appointment

All types of Dancing taught . Tap and Acrobatic a Speciality
Personal attention given to each pupil

DISPLAYS will be given throughout the
year at Garden Parties, Charity Shows
——————— and Pantomimes ———————

MISS NOBLE will be pleased to give her assistance to any Charity
upon application to her or to Mrs. Findlay at "Lyndale,"
Bromsgrove Road, Hunnington. Telephone: HALesowen 1460

An advertisement for Miss Eva Noble's Paramount School of Dancing.

six

The War Years

Hole in my bucket

I attended Woodhouse Road School. Early in the war, shelters were in the playground.

We went there occasionally for practice drills. I remember it being very dark and gloomy inside with benches along the long walls and down the centre. My guess is that they used hand-lamps as lighting, as candles would have been too dangerous. We used to sing, 'There's a hole in my bucket, dear Liza' – obviously we weren't wearing our gas masks.

I would imagine this was meant to speed the exodus from the classrooms to the shelters without having to panic and to get everyone used to the atmosphere in the shelters. Occasionally in class we wore our gas masks for a short time. I didn't like it! One of the two wooden classrooms was mine in 1941.

I remember attending school half-day. I went in the mornings and was very peeved that my cousin Barbara Martin, also from Glyn Farm Road, could stay in bed later because she went to the afternoon session. I assumed that our part-time schooling was due to a lot of the male teachers having joined the forces.

Stella Linnington

Stockings and servicemen

Older girls and young women, finding stockings unobtainable, bought a substance from the chemist, a brownish liquid, which they painted on their legs. Getting both legs the same shade was, I was led to understand, rather difficult; also the substance rubbing off on the bedclothes was a problem to be faced. There were occasions when sand and water, when thoroughly mixed, was the means of providing the required leg colour.

A dark coloured pencil was sometimes used to draw the seam of the stocking on the coloured leg. This required an artistic expertise that was usually beyond most people. The problem was eventually solved when American servicemen were stationed in the area and nylon stockings became readily available.

Denis Colclough

'Douse that light!'

From Birch Road opposite the shops on the corner of White Road in the central reservation was an air-raid shelter; as soon as the sirens went a lot of people used to take all that they needed in a wooden box. Sometimes when the air raid started and it was bad, the buses would park up in Birch Road and the drivers and conductors would take some of the seats out of the bus down the shelter for the people to sit on. A lot of people wouldn't go down the shelter; they said they might as well die in the comfort of their own homes. The shelters were Anderson shelters, you had to dig a big hole in your garden and then put this shelter in and then cover it over with turf. The ARP wardens came round and would shout, 'Douse that light!' even if there was just a crack of light showing.

Lawrence Basterfield

Bad air raid

I recall a bad raid in Birmingham. I was at The Odeon, the organ came up and the film stopped but then everyone left when the 'all clear' was heard. I walked to the Town Hall because the buses only went to the Town Hall, got on the bus and the sirens started again, so they took us all to what used to be Greys and I was there till four o'clock in the morning. We would walk home from Birmingham and think nothing of it.

Irene Devereux

Pupils on local farms

My husband John remembers his school days at Four Dwellings senior mixed school. During the war years, pupils were allowed to work on the local farms, Merris's and Beckett's, during school hours. Beckett's was situated by The Monarch public house on Quinton Road West. They were given a card with twenty half-day allowances, the farmer would mark off the card when they worked, mainly at picking potatoes – for this they were paid 5d per hour. John can also remember a plane crashing during the war in the field to the right as you go up Ridgacre Lane towards the school.

During the war, a barrage balloon was tethered in a field situated in Green Lane/Ridgacre Lane and Ridgacre Road on the site of the post office sorting depot. At the end of the war, when servicemen were moved off the site, the Nissen huts were taken over by squatters. I believe this was one way of getting priority for a council house when they became available. During the war Corporation buses were parked overnight on the hill of Ridgacre Road down towards World's End Lane, which at that time was only a one-track unfinished lane, to avoid any direct bombing on the garages destroying their vehicles.

Mrs Sheila Joyner

Evacuation

When in 1941 the suggestion of evacuation for Quinton children arose, my parents decided it would be safer for me to go. They expected the destination to be Bridgnorth or some place reasonably accessible. They were not told the destination until the bus arrived at the school to pick us up at the start of our journey – to South Wales! We were accompanied by teachers who travelled with us and stayed long enough to see that we all had foster-parents, and deal with any problems which arose. The bus took us to a railway station, probably Snow Hill, then we travelled to Crumlin, a mining village in Monmouthshire, where they had no air raids at all.

We had a short walk from the station to the school where food had been prepared for us. Afterwards, prospective foster-parents advanced and made their choice. I remember one group of four sisters had to be split; Iris, the eldest, and the youngest went to one home and the other two went to another. The first two went home quite soon, but the other two stayed on.

The houses in the village were mostly modest-sized terraced houses, built into the hillsides, so it was very generous of the people to take in so many unknown children.

In the village, before we arrived, relations of my foster-parents had taken in two sisters- Edna and Joyce Walker – from Nechells. I never enquired how that was arranged. My foster-parents already had my foster-mother's parents living with them and they had two small shops in the village, so they had a busy life before accepting me to live with them. Our parents paid a weekly sum towards our keep and it was passed to the relevant host families.

On our arrival in the village, the local children mocked us evacuees for our Brummie accents, but we were soon accepted and made friends with each other. We all had to make adjustments. In about six months or so, we too spoke with a Welsh accent. We were lucky that it was an English-speaking area and we didn't have to learn to speak Welsh.

I was nine years old and this was all a great shock to the system. I'd had no idea what to expect. I was an only child and had always been well cared for and went to my parents with any problems. I was lucky that my foster-parents looked after me well and with affection.

Most of the year, my only contact with my parents was by letter. My father posted a letter to me every Monday enclosing pocket money. It arrived every Tuesday, except on about three occasions when it arrived a day late – and this in almost four years of wartime conditions. I wrote back to them every other Tuesday. They came to visit me the only times they could – for about three days at Easter and a week in August.

Mrs Stella Linnington

Fire-watching for adults

Street lights were either very dimly lit or not lit at all and the few motor vehicles that were allowed petrol had their headlights obliterated by a black shield except for a very narrow horizontal slot which allowed a thin dim light to escape. Going out after dark to assist the air-raid warden with her stirrup pump, bucket of water or bucket of sand to extinguish incendiary bombs was an exciting time for some youngsters. Joining a fire-watching team, however, was an activity restricted to adults.

Following an air raid it was usual for boys to search the streets for shrapnel. This was any small fragment of metal remains of anti-aircraft shells, which had disintegrated and fallen to the ground after being fired at the enemy aircraft. Occasionally it would be possible to find parts of an incendiary bomb; this scrap metal

had no intrinsic value but its collection became a craze amongst boys that rivalled the collection of marbles or cigarette cards.

Iron railings surrounding public buildings and parks were removed and used for the war effort. This resulted in many parks, which had formerly had their gates locked at a prescribed time by the park keeper, being readily accessible at all hours. The social consequences of this can be imagined.

At this time, lorries regularly toured the streets and people were requested to donate metal implements, particularly aluminium saucepans and frying pans, to be melted down to provide the material to build aircraft.

Denis Colclough

Allotment supplements

I was ten years old when war broke out in September 1939. I lived with my parents in Ridgacre Road next to the Christadelphian Church and opposite what is now the Quinborne Centre. We were all issued with identity cards and gas masks, which we had to take everywhere with us. The school roll call included 'gasmask', just to be sure we had it with us.

It was very dark in the streets and a torch was essential when you went out at night. No. 8 batteries were always in short supply, along with most other things.

Quite early in the war my father rented an allotment; there were about seven in the triangle of land between Ridgacre Road and Quinton Lane, now covered in houses. The vegetables he grew were a welcome supplement to the meagre rations; I really don't know how mothers catered for their families; fish paste sandwiches featured quite frequently. We also kept about half a dozen hens in the back garden and for most of the year they laid well and kept us supplied with eggs. My mother used to preserve any surplus in water glass in a large bucket for when the hens moulted and went off laying.

Nora Hyett

I found a German medal

I'm an old Quintonian who lived in Newburn Croft off Highfield Lane. When I was eleven, in 1954, I was playing cricket with tennis rackets in the fields opposite where we lived.

I found a German medal lying in the grass and being a well-trained young lad took it home to my dad who said, 'You'd better take it to the police station and see if anyone claims it.'

No one claimed it, so out of curiosity off I went to the museum and art gallery in Birmingham. They didn't know anything about it but sent it off to the Imperial War Museum in London for identification.

Eventually it returned identified as a Nazi Germany war decoration awarded to foreigners for distinguished service in the war on behalf of the Third Reich.

W. Price

Hair care

During the war one could not buy shampoo, conditioners or perms. Most girls grew their hair long and took great care of their crowning glory. Hair was washed with the mildest soap available and rainwater from the water butt was used. It made the hair soft.

Brown and auburn-haired girls rinsed their hair with beer to feed the hair, heighten the colour and give it gloss. Blond hair was rinsed with lemon juice or a beaten egg. To lighten blond hair, one rinsed it with a heavy salt and water solution and dried it in the sun. This bleached the hair and the salt was carefully rinsed out afterwards. Setting lotion was made with a solution of sugar and water.

If the scalp was flakey, it could be cleared by rinsing the hair with water that had had nettles boiled in it. It was massaged into the scalp.

To get a straight, sleek hairstyle, curly hair was ironed straight through a damp cloth. When curls were in fashion they could be created in many ways. Metal curling tongs were heated in the fire or in the gas stove jets and tested on newspaper until it no longer singed the paper. The ends of a lock of hair were wound around the rounded tong and secured by the hollow tong, scissor fashion, the rest was rolled round the closed tongs up to the head and held there until it was curly enough and the tongs had cooled a little. Also used as curlers were pipe cleaners, twisted paper strips or rag strips

Mrs Charlotte Tate (*née* Masters)

Wireless threats

In Quinton during the war, we were on rations. Some of us worked at the Birmetals and we were on war work; we were always well fed, it was 2d for soup, 9d for dinner and 3d for sweet. We got 4s for fire-watching, once a month on a rota, so we were out one night every month. At night you could listen to Lord Haw Haw on the wireless, he would say, 'I know where you all are, I know where the Birmetals and Austin factory is, we'll get you!'

One Saturday night and Sunday morning we were awoken by terrible noises – one of the barrage balloons had come loose; it had knocked nineteen chimney pots off and landed somewhere on the Wolverhampton Road. Lawrence Basterfield's dad had the post office and had to take messages.

Mrs Joan Smith (*née* Clay)

Our saviours

Each morning, after there had been an air raid, before setting out to school at the Quinton Church of England School, I would go out on to the lawn to search for pieces of shrapnel. When I met my friends at school, we would compare our shrapnel to see who had picked up the largest piece.

Our pilots would fly over Quinton either training or enemy plane spotting. When one of them flew over the school at playtime, we would all wave to the crew. They were not very high up by modern standards. Once one of the pilots waved a white scarf at us in reply. It was such a thrill. We regarded these men as our knights in shining armour. Our saviours. They were.

Many of my peers had fathers who were fighting abroad. Some of these fathers did not return alas. I remember wounded fathers at home on leave coming to meet their children from school. They wore special clothes; a royal blue suit and forage cap, a red tie and a white shirt. One of these men had his arm in a sling.

As more and more of the young men were called up into the armed forces, several young Quinton couples brought their wedding dates forward in order to be married before the men were sent abroad. One of these young war brides, a neighbour's daughter, married her pilot sweetheart. They had a two-day honeymoon, and then one week later he was killed.

Mrs Charlotte Tate (*née* Masters)

A bombed house

I was six and a half years old when my home was bombed during a very bad raid over Birmingham. Mother always said that it was during the night of the longest raid over the city but there might be a little doubt on this date; anyway it was at the end of November or early December in 1940.

My sister and I had not been taken to the air-raid shelter on that particular night as we were both suffering from whooping cough and Mother did not want us in the night air. However, the raid worsened and she became increasingly uneasy. Just about 8.30 p.m. she heard a man's voice: 'Madge, take those children to the shelter – now!' Mother thought it was our father; he was an ARP who would call in when he was patrolling the road. After investigating, no one else was found in the house, but we were wrapped up warm and taken to the shelter.

Towards 9.30 p.m. Dad came back to the house with Jack James, his partner that night. They had come to the shelter to check if we were alright, but Mr James became uneasy by the force of the raid and checked to see if his wife was safe in the shelter. He had got in the right of way when a gun which was located on the Tennal School playing field, together with a barrage balloon, hit a plane. Four bombs dropped, one on Brunner's sweet shop, killing Mrs Brunner and her son who were in the shelter, the second at the back of our house on the allotments, the third bomb dropped directly on our house leaving a 30ft crater, the final one fell on the grass verge in front of our house.

I can remember the woman in the shelter next door screaming and also recall the terrible smell of gas; however, we were all remarkably calm in our shelter. I expect our parents knew what had happened but tried to protect us. The next thing I knew was a fireman coming through the door with an axe and carried my sister and I out. Quite a time must have elapsed between getting us out of the shelter and the bomb hitting the house because there were such a lot of people about: the doctor, the vicar and some boys from Tennal School who had been escorted up by a master to see if they could help.

Everyone was so kind; there was a rest centre at Woodhouse Road School and we were asked to go there but my mother refused. However, a neighbour took us in for a week or two until we could be sorted out. Clothes, curtains etc. were strung about the trees but virtually nothing remained of our lovely home. All we had were the clothes we stood up in. Dad rang his works the next morning and said he couldn't come in as he had to find accommodation and clothes for us but he was actually asked if he could get in by lunchtime! (I never knew what my father's reply was).

Mr Salt, a gentleman from St Faith's Church, who had a car (almost unknown in those days) took my sister and I down to Harper's in Albany Road in Harborne and told Miss Harper to clothe us in whatever we needed.

Dad also caught a man sorting through the debris; when he was challenged he claimed to be one of the helpers but when searched, my mother's engagement ring, which had somehow survived, was found in his pocket. I never discovered what happened to him but to steal from us when we had nothing left was a bit sad to say the least.

Everyone else was good to us; a lady in Fitzroy Avenue gave us a Christmas tree, another lady from Wolverhampton Road South gave us the trimmings and the Baptist church in Harborne sent us a children's tea service to play with. I remember it had red handles.

Later on, the Lord Mayor of Birmingham gave a party for the children of the city who had been bombed or those whose fathers were prisoners of war. I thought it was very grand and we came away with a large bag of sweets so I thought it was almost worth it.

Mrs D. Timms

A salvage officer

Housewives had to return to work whether they wanted to or not. My mother and others like her who had small children or babies were not expected to go to work but were given work to do at home. My mother became the salvage officer for our road. Large sacks were delivered to our house and hooked over the fence beside our drive. All the neighbours would deposit their waste paper and cardboard into these sacks. We were given a large, white-painted tin. This was delivered and kept on our front door step. It was a bone tin. The neighbours had to deposit their meat bones in this tin. I do not know what these bones were used for, but all this salvage was collected twice a week.

New, clean, shiny dustbins were put at intervals all down the road. Left-over food of every description was to be put in these bins. We were told that these leftovers were boiled up and fed to the pigs.

Mrs Charlotte Tate (née Masters)

A brave soul

During the war my sister was always a brave soul, especially with the incendiary bombs. You had this long-handled shovel and a bucket of sand. It was so ridiculous really. We were told that if an incendiary bomb came down outside the house in the road, to take off the lid from the dustbin and place it over the bomb. I can't believe we were told to do this and even more so that we actually did it. When I think about it, we must have been quite mad. The chap next door was quite kind and because we were all women, most of the men being at war, after a raid he would come in to see if we were alright. One day they must have thought that the Odeon cinema was a factory and they dropped a string of incendiaries on it. Well one went through the bedroom ceiling and my sister, not to be daunted, dashes upstairs with her long-handled shovel, scoops it up and throws it out through the window. Well! Just at that moment the man next door, Mr Hillyard, was walking through the gate to check if we were alright, just as this incendiary bomb flew past him. The air was quite blue as he cried: 'That's bloody marvellous that is; I come to check if you are alright and you throw a bomb at me!'

Mrs Eileen Lee (*née* Clark)

VE Day came

The years passed, and life was tedious rather than dangerous; the worst aspect of it was the shortages of food – fruit, but especially clothing. Our siren suits were made of Army surplus blankets and occasionally there was parachute silk to make underwear. Stockings

had to be darned to make them last as long as possible. In about 1945, a few lucky girls obtained nylons from American boyfriends.

D-Day had happened and I remember standing on the front doorsteps and watching wave after wave of aircraft heading south. At last VE Day came and there were street parties and bonfires.

Nora Hyett

Quinton's Home Guard

I was nine years and one month old when the war started and remember hearing the announcement on the wireless. From then on, at least for the first year of the war, my main memories are of Dad joining the Home Guard 'on our side of the road'. He had a local defence volunteer armband at first and then a

VE Day celebrations at Edenhall Road on 8 May 1945.

Barston Road street party held in 1945.

Home Guard uniform. I seem to have spent a lot of time with him and his colleagues – all very local men, of course, and remember their guardroom being a building, which is still there, further up the road from home.

It had previously been a Co-op shop. It seems to have been unused for ages but is now let as retail premises. It is one storey and next to the barbers. The Home Guard equipment was very sparse at first but the men seemed cheerful. They also did guard duties overnight in the Danilo cinema. I remember Dad letting me into the cinema through an exit to the

upstairs seats to see Greta Garbo in *Ninotchka*. I didn't enjoy it as I was sure I would be seen and get into trouble.

The headquarters of the platoon was a house called High Tor at the top of Perry Hill Road where Colonel Fillery held sway. He was a sweet manufacturer for Fillerys Toffees, as was Bill Tyler, Ernest's Mintoes. Other Home Guards I particularly remember were Ernie Atack and Bill Salisbury who both lived on Hagley Road West, our side of course. Reg Salisbury, one of Bill's sons, spent some of the war on the *Ark Royal*.

Quinton Home Guard Battalion officers seated outside the headquarters in Perry Hill Road in October 1944.

Dad went to a Home Guard camp one weekend – held in the Illey area. While he was away there was a knock on our door late on Saturday night. It was a Canadian soldier who had missed the last bus into Birmingham. Amazingly, mother let him stay the night. After he'd gone the next morning I cycled to the Home Guard camp to tell dad our exciting news. There was a young lad on guard who challenged me in the usual way –'Halt! Who goes there?' I thought this rather silly at the time as the answer seemed obvious. I was admitted and told my story. Mother worked at home taking orders and payments for Baggeridge Coal and a large sign, illuminated except in wartime, at our front gate proclaimed 'Buy Baggeridge Coal'. This may have attracted the Canadian to our house.

Mrs Marjorie Berry (née Phillips)

Two German pilots

The Home Guard had the greengrocers during the war; they also used the Danilo. One night, a plane was shot down over Blackheath and two German pilots were captured by the Home Guard and taken to the greengrocers. During the war, they had a land mine dropped at the old men's home and everyone had to evacuate the area. We were moved to Blackheath but you could see them carrying the old men on stretchers and wheelchairs and taking them to the Danilo in the middle of the night.

Lawrence Basterfield

Suddenly the world changed

I was three years of age when war broke out on 3 September 1939; then the world changed suddenly for the young and old alike.

One of my uncles, William Breakwell, a railwayman by day, joined the Home Guard. It was exciting to see him with black shoe polish on his face, going out on night exercises, carrying his rifle.

Houses stopped being built. The street lamps were turned off. Petrol was rationed and only sold to people who needed their cars for business purposes.

My grandparents, who ran the Ansells Outdoor in High Street, were advised to use their cellars as shelter from the bombs.

Barrage balloons appeared in the sky over Quinton. They were supposed to stop low-flying enemy aircraft I think. They looked like glossy, grey elephants, rocking and swaying in the breeze. There was one anchored to a great iron ring, set in concrete, in a field close to Wiggins sports ground.

Mrs Charlotte Tate (*née* Masters)

REME camp

There was a REME camp near Ridgacre Lane where the soldiers lived in Nissen huts. They worked in the garage near the Hollybush. Eventually they had some Italian prisoners with them and they were allowed to wander around Quinton as the end of the war came in sight. We girls were interested in them as they seemed so different and lads of our age group who we would normally have talked to were away in the forces. We followed them around and learnt Italian songs. They were a lot older than us and some were undoubtedly married men with families back home, but

Arthur and Charlotte Masters outside the Ansells Outdoor in the High Street in 1922.

REME camp on the corner of Ridgacre Lane and Green Lane on 8 May 1945.

since other people ignored them, they were glad to talk to us and treated us well. I have a photo of myself and two friends with five of them in the field behind the REME camp on VE Day 1945. I was fourteen.

Dad did not like the Italians and I think he regarded them as cowards. But strangely he would talk to German prisoners we met on holiday and gave them cigarettes. Dad had been a soldier in the First World War and was forty-six when the Second World War started.

There was an auxiliary fire station on our side of the road nearer the Hollybush, where the Texaco garage is now, and I remember being rolled up in deep snow with my friends by some firemen. I felt most uncomfortable going home with wet snow everywhere.

Mrs Marjorie Berry (*née* Phillips)

Pigs to pork

My grandparents, Arthur and Charlotte Masters, had always kept pigs from the time they came to live and work in Quinton in 1908 and then onwards right through the war years. They purchased their piglets in pairs usually and whether the pigs were male or female they were always named Dennis and Ginny. They were very well fed. My grandparents would say, 'If you put nothing in the sty, you will get nothing out of it'. The pigs were reared in one of the two stables in the garden of the Ansells outdoor. They were always very clean, brushed, petted and kept happy. They would snuggle down in deep straw and grunt softly to one another.

Contrary to popular belief, pigs like to be clean. They did not foul their deep, clean straw but, like a pet guinea pig, would use one corner of the stable for a toilet. There was a gutter in the brick-built floor there and their waste was hosed along this gutter and into the drain outside. John Masters, the youngest of the Masters family, was a butcher and would kill the pigs. The bladder was washed, then blown up with a bicycle pump and the neck tied with string, and we children would play ball with it. Nothing was wasted, it seems; my granny used to say: 'the only thing on a pig that you could not use was its squeal'.

Mrs Charlotte Tate (*née* Masters)

The trial rocket launcher

At the outbreak of war, the Royal Engineers set up a searchlight detachment at Howley Grange Farm which was on the land now occupied by Howley Grange School. This detachment consisted of a searchlight together with its own generator unit, a sound locator, and a Lewis machine gun. This little outfit consisted of a total of ten men, which included a sergeant and a lance corporal. So with time on my hands, I used to run errands for these men to the local shops. Needless to say, most of the errands were to Dad's shop, which was a nice little earner for him.

Just after the searchlight moved in, there was another defence unit in the shape of a barrage balloon. This was moored in an adjacent field just behind where Wiggins recreation ground used to be then. I would imagine that the M5 motorway now encompasses all of that little lot. I also ran errands for the RAF crew who manned the balloon site.

This balloon once broke loose from its mooring cable and drifted across the area, finally coming to rest across the roofs of two houses in Howley Grange Road. The searchlight was used along with many more round the city during most of the night-time raids

on the city, but I never remember the machine gun being put to use. There were no heavy anti-aircraft guns in the neighbourhood; most of these were on the other side of the city and I've no idea why that was. The German bombers used to navigate on Bartley Green reservoir and then lay a line of parachute flares into the city.

There was however a trial rocket launcher site situated over at Stonehouse near Harborne. This was used once; we heard an approaching bomber, then there was this awful rushing sort of noise, followed by explosions, which seemed to go on for ages. When all that noise had abated, we could still hear the same bomber droning on towards the city. One could imagine the crew giving some sort of salute to the rocket gun crews!

Clive Davies

The pig club

My parents moved to Apsley Road in June 1939 just before the outbreak of the Second World War.

I was just five years old. Because of the outbreak of war, all building of houses stopped abruptly and there were still fields and farmland opposite our house. The road was unmade – just yellow gravel with blue bricks poking through. I never seemed to have my knees free from scratches and bruises. We did, however, have pavements where we spent hours playing hopscotch.

Anderson shelters were dug in the gardens and we kept three chickens in a pen to get eggs.

At the back of the houses was a piece of rough ground which was turned into allotments and a group of residents from Apsley Road and Kingsway joined together to form a pig club. Three or four sties were built to house the pigs and a shed to house the boiler

Apsley Road pig club.

for brewing the pig swill and a dry place to store the straw for bedding.

My father had a motorbike and sidecar, which he used to collect scraps from the householders who were encouraged to use the bins, which were placed in the right-of-ways between the roads. He was allocated a special petrol coupon allowance for this. The site is still there and is used for allotments to this day – called the Tinkers Farm Allotment Association.

Vivienne Harris (*née* Jacomb)

We queued for bananas

A date which sticks in my memory was Tuesday 11 September 1945; it was to be my first day at George Dixon Grammar School. It was also the day of the first allocation of bananas after the war. My mother walked to Stanley Road with me; I stood in the no. 9 bus queue whilst my mother stood in the queue for bananas. She got them just before the bus came and I was allowed to take a whole banana to school. I was the envy of my classmates, and subsequent allocations of bananas were cut up and shared between us – those were the days!

Bryan Palser

A POW camp

When I was a lad, the Welsh House Farm was Richards' farm and during the war it was used as a prisoner of war camp; some of the first there were Spanish prisoners from the Spanish Civil War. When the war started, the Germans formed a Blue Division, which were made up of Spaniards from the Spanish Civil War. We caught a few in France before Dunkirk and they ended up in this POW Camp at Welsh House Farm. Then it was full of Germans in about 1946; there were no SS men – they were all conscripts and a lot of them were quite old. Some didn't join till the Ardennes; some were called up at the end of the war when they were calling up the older men and the boys. They just waited for the first chance to surrender, spent a time in POW camps then went back to Germany in 1947.

We used to go and play football with them; they laid out a football pitch. You could walk from where Tom Powell's farm was; there was a path along there down to Welsh House Farm and there was a flat piece on the top that they made into a football pitch. There was a bomb disposal squad at Tennal Grange. A chap called Snowy White ran a football team which used to play these Germans and we used to play them as well when I was only about sixteen or seventeen; we had some good times

there. There was about 300 to 400 there. No security there, barbed wire or anything, in fact a lot of them worked on the farms. Near the Stonehouse Farm in Stonehouse Lane was a battery of rocket guns. There was a barrage balloon in Queens Park and Selly Park and we used to help the four WAFFs put the balloon up but the Germans kept shooting it down. We played football in Queens Park so we used to help the WAFFs put the balloon up about half an hour before darkness. We would take the ratchets off and the balloon would go up by itself, the hard part was winding it in, especially on a windy day.

They misfired the first shell and it came down and hit the gable wall of the house on the corner of Wentworth Park Avenue. In fact today you can still see the new bricks in the gable facing Lordswood Road.

John Birch

Seeing Coventry burn

A vivid memory from the 1939 war was when a land mine was dropped near the cottages. We all spent the night at Clent but my mum said: 'In the morning we are going home; if we're going to die, we may as well all die together'. We crept under the barriers, whilst the police shouted 'You fools – remember not to light the gas and have the windows open'. I stood with my father on the front door step in November 1940; I think I had my father's helmet on my head. He was an air-raid warden, my dad, after work. He said to me: 'When you are older you will say that you saw Coventry burn'– the sky was a bright orange-yellow.

Miss Gladys Jones

Father had been at the Somme

My father was a regimental sergeant major during the First World War and he had been

Left Ammunition boxes being made at Smith Bros, Quinton, in the 1940s.

Opposite Utility clothing label.

at the Somme. He actually got gassed but he was fortunate because he was quite healthy until he was about sixty-five. He caught a bad case of 'flu and in the doctors words it caused the gas to start moving and that's really what killed him, although the death certificate read 'bronchitis and pneumonia'; I remember reading at the time that quite a few men were dying of the same thing.

Mrs Eileen Lee (*née* Clark)

An order of ammunition

When we first started out on our own, we wanted to get a contract for ammunition boxes, as it was such good business. This pal of Ran's, Cyril Goodway, and then another friend, a chap named Wilf Scutt called Scutty, got us a job for the Ministry of Supply.

Scutty arranged for this chap, Colonel Van den Berg, and a chap named Green, who did all the work, to come and see us. Anyway he came along, and he gave us an order for 50,000 new ammunition boxes

Cliff Smith and Smith Bros Family Archives

Utility goods

The hardships and shortages continued, particularly fuel and electricity in the terrible winter of 1947. Food was severely rationed when I got married in 1950.

One bright thing for teenage girls was the end of clothes rationing in about 1947 and the coming of the new look. We all acquired longer and fuller skirts after the austerity of wartime clothing. I should also mention utility goods, clothes, household linens and furniture etc. – plain but serviceable and they all helped over the next few years.

Nora Hyett

Other local titles published by Tempus

Birmingham Cinemas
CHRISTINE WILKINSON AND MARGARET HANSON

Through the medium of old photographs, advertisements and programmes, this book provides a nostalgic look at the history of cinema-going in the city of Birmingham, from its early beginning as a fairground attraction right up to the present day and the giant multiplex cinema. This volume is sure to appeal to those who remember visiting some of the now long-gone movie houses, and anyone else with an interest in the architectural and social history of Birmingham.
0 7524 3080 7

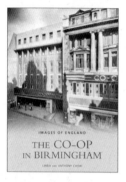

The Co-op in Birmingham
LINDA AND ANTHONY CHEW

Few retail organisations have had such an effect on people's lives and have offered such a wide range of services as 'the Co-op'. This collection of archive photographs illustrates just how diverse and all-embracing the Birmingham Co-operative Society was. We see the full scope of its activities, from grocery shops to department stores, dairy deliveries to funeral services and, for both members and staff, a wide range of benefits and social pursuits.
0 7524 3098 X

The Inner Circle Birmingham's No.8 Bus Route
MARGARET HANSON, DAVID HARVEY AND PETER DRAKE

This collection of over 200 archive images will appeal to those who have travelled the inner circle route or who simply have an interest in the history of Birmingham. The scenes and buses reveal just how much times have changed, while the informative captions remind us of a different era. This was a time when conductors would actually escort young passengers from the bus to their front door.
0 7524 2636 2

Bullring The Heart of Birmingham
MICHAEL HALLETT AND PETER JAMES

This book is a contemporary archive of a dramatic change in the city of Birmingham. It celebrates the construction of the Bullring with unique photographs and panoramic images by Michael Hallett, and records a captivating phase in the vision for a new Birmingham – Europe's largest city centre regeneration project. It reviews the Bullring's growth from a hole in the ground to the glorious unfolding of the final stages.
0 7524 3041 6

If you are interested in purchasing other books published by Tempus, or in case you have difficulty finding any Tempus books in your local bookshop, you can also place orders directly through our website
www.tempus-publishing.com